D0917515

TENAFLY PUBLIC LIBRARY
DISCARD

ESL Shakespeare: 101 Everyday Phrases

Martin Jago

Smith and Kraus Publishers

ISBN 9781575258645
Library of Congress Control Number: 2013948483

Typesetting and layout by Elizabeth E. Monteleone
Cover by: Borderlands Press
Photo by Isar Jamalpour—www.isarphotography.com

A Smith and Kraus book
177 Lyme Road, Hanover, NH 03755
editorial 603.643.6431 To Order 1.877.668.8680
www.smithandkraus.com

To Colonel Brian James and his most esteemed wife Christine
(My dear mum and dad)

O Lord that lends me life,
Lend me a heart replete with thankfulness.
Henry VI, Part 2, Act I, sc. i

Acknowledgments

Thank you to Janet Rosen and Sheree Bykofsky for their support, advice, and guidance.

My gratitude to Marisa Smith, and everyone at Smith and Kraus for their hard work and dedication as always.

My sincerest gratitude to Robert Filback at USC's Rossier School of Education. The insightful words, wisdom, and humor that he shares in the generous foreword to this book are excellent.

Thank you to photographer Isar Jamalpour at www.isarphotography.com for his consummate professionalism, good humor, and for being an excellent tennis partner who in the spirit of good sportsmanship allows me to win the occasional point.

To those teachers, educators, writers and students who freely gave their time and shared their thoughts on various early drafts and to those who at a later stage provided endorsements (Carol V Davis, Richard Perkins, Mitch Karpp, Joanna Benitez, Ellie Zhang and Andrea Fredricks) I sincerely thank you.

Thanks to Sheila McCracken for your encouragement.

Thanks also to Andrew Allen-King, Kim and Ames for being there from the outset of my LA journey and providing their fair share of love and laughter. Much appreciated.

To my family, thank you all, not least mum, dad, big brother Tim, and my grandmother, Phyllis Rogers.

Finally, my love and gratitude always to Nicola Bertram and Sunee James, a long-suffering duo (wife and son) who inspire me, encourage me, and sustain me through thick and thin again and again.

Contents

Foreword

Early in my profession as an English language teacher, I spent a year working with high school students in a small city in Transylvania—a beautifully lush and refreshingly remote region of Romania. This was the early nineties, so foreign English teachers in Romania were somewhat novel—as were contemporary English language teaching materials! Since the postal system was a bit unreliable, anything we wanted to teach with, we had to carry in ourselves. Imagine my surprise when I spot among the materials brought by a fellow American teacher a single volume edition of Shakespeare's complete works! Since my appreciation for Shakespeare was less developed then, my reaction did not reflect teaching concerns—"Wow, what an awesome addition to our teaching library!"—but logistical matters—"Dude, that must weigh five pounds! What were you thinking?!" Compelling my colleague to lug over a massive Shakespeare text was an insight that I now share—and a truth that has certainly guided Martin Jago in his work as a director, playwright, and author. What is it? This: Shakespeare is a rich and utterly essential encounter for anyone interested in the English language—especially teachers and learners of English.

With this book, Martin has created an accessible and valuable resource to help integrate Shakespeare into our teaching and learning of English. Drawing on a career working with Shakespeare in the theatre, he has identified a wealth of everyday phrases and idioms that originated with Shakespeare—*fight fire with fire, in a pickle, wild goose chase* and 98 others. The book will not only offer light, supplementary material for intermediate to advanced level students, it will also provide exposure to some of the practical, everyday language that animates English conversations around the world. For teachers wanting to help their students increase communicative competence, a clever strategy is to draw their attention to the common currency certain phrases and idioms have in everyday speech. Imagine an English learner who is able to quip seamlessly how "*brevity is the soul of wit*," or able to interject in a discussion that "it appears we've *come full circle*!"

This book really shines in its practical application and usability for teachers. This reflects Martin's additional experience as a former ESL teacher of adults. He has supported each phrase or idiom with a definition, an example narrative, and a short dialogue to provide practice and to help contextualize it. With the busy teacher in mind, they have been arranged alphabetically and interspersed with ready-to-use quizzes. Finally, a reference to the original Shakespeare source for each phrase or idiom offers a nifty tool for introducing students to the actual texts. This last feature gets us back to the real value of this book and the driving passion of its author. Shakespeare is worth getting into. His enduring impact on modern English, down to this day, and the inherently poetic nature of his words are reason enough to incorporate a bit of the Bard of Avon into our teaching. Similar to my colleague's decision decades ago, this book of Shakespeare is one to bring along.

Robert A. Filback, Ph.D.
Associate Professor of Clinical Education
Rossier School of Education
University of Southern California

Introduction

Learning English is not, to borrow from the Immortal Bard, for the "faint-hearted." In many ways, ours is a language of broken rules where we learn the grammar only to undo it by way of countless exceptions.

Then there's the vocabulary. There are more words in English than any other language in the world, and as for pronunciation, just don't look at the spelling for clues in this area. If that weren't enough to cope with, there are also things like phrasal verbs and idioms to tackle.

For example, take the phrasal verb, "run out." Here's an example of its usage:

"Oh dear, my pen has just run out!"

Encountering this verb in the given context for the first time, the English student scratches his head and does all he can to make sense of it, perhaps conjuring an image of the pen sprouting legs and dashing from the room. It really is a hopeless cause. The same is true of idioms. "Break the ice" actually means to make a person feel at ease. As with the phrasal verb, the idiom bears no relation to the literal meaning of the words. The only thing to do with such phrases is commit their meaning to memory; a task easier said than done.

If you're wondering what all this has to do with Shakespeare, read on Macduff.

Introducing literature to language students is a noble idea but aside from the grammar rules and vocabulary, most students want to grasp the kind of everyday language they're likely to hear in the supermarket, coffee shop or standing in a queue at the bank.

Thankfully, many of the common phrases and idioms used today come to us directly from Shakespeare.

It's not often that high-brow classical literature, and language of the 21st century come together in one place, but such was Shakespeare's influence on the language that this unique book is able to marry the two in a neat and accessible way that is fun, informative, and educational.

ESL Shakespeare: 101 Everyday Phrases is aimed at students from intermediate to advanced levels of study and can be used in many ways. The book will help build new vocabulary and introduce students to a variety of grammar topics.

As a teacher, you might decide to make *ESL Shakespeare* a regular feature of the classroom. As a student, you may simply wish to study at your own leisure and pace.

Either way, the self-contained units that follow make the book equally suited to readers who choose a cover to cover approach, and those who prefer to dip in randomly.

Each unit includes a phrase, reference to Shakespeare source, a phrase definition and examples that contextualize the phrase in a short, prose narrative, and a brief A/B dialogue.

Practicing the exercises out loud is strongly advised. Partner work on the dialogue section will aid the development of good listening skills and give students valuable speech and pronunciation practice.

Throughout the book you'll find a series of *Quick Quizzes* and at the back of the book, the *Quick List*. These resources provide a handy reference and great way to check student learning. Additional features include the sample dialogue, *A Tale of Love, Betrayal, and the English Language*. It's a bit of lighthearted fun that puts to use more than half the 101 phrases you can find in this book, demonstrating the everyday use that such phrases can play in a simple conversation between two friends.

The dialogue is followed by a ten minute ESL version of *Romeo and Juliet*, and a modern translation of Shakespeare's most famous sonnet, *Shall I compare thee to a summer's day?*

These additional components help to further strengthen and build the ESL learner's English skills with the help of the English language's most venerated writer.

By highlighting the commonly used, practical English that we English speakers use every day of our lives, Shakespeare is harnessed throughout this book for ESL purposes, bridging the gap between literature and the practical application of the English language.

The use of idioms and everyday phrases such as the ones contained in this book vary from English-speaking country to English-speaking country (you may be familiar with the old quip about the Britain and America being *two nations divided by a common language*).

Indeed, like twins separated shortly after birth and now living quite separate lives on either side of the Atlantic, we find as many shared traits as nurtured ones: two branches of the same tree which stem from the same roots, and grow in their own unique way.

Accordingly, idioms and common expressions fall in and out of fashion throughout the English-speaking world and at different times and places. While some idiomatic expressions never seem to lose their appeal regardless of how well-worn they might be, others may feel clichéd or overdone.

Howbeit, at their very best, a commonly used idiom or turn of phrase can lend a ready and eloquent simplicity to human expression.

Maybe you are simply looking for some light relief from the rigors of grammar practice, in which case I hope this humble tome provides the relief while serving as a useful supplement to any course of ESL study.

Some of the 101 expressions contained in this book have a distinctly British flavor and in some cases their use would be out of place in American English. You'll find notes highlighting uniquely British phrases and where possible I have included common American equivalents or phrasal alternatives. I felt it important to include such phrases because besides providing idioms from the English-speaking world as a whole, much of our 21st century cultural experience is through movies and television programs. Consequently, English language learners are just as likely to hear uniquely British phrases as they are those more common to American English.

In many instances, Shakespeare is credited with giving the English language its first recorded case of the phrases and idioms contained in this book. However, which of those phrases he invented from scratch, which ones he borrowed (perhaps from other languages or spoken usage) and which ones he changed or modified from existing models, is hard to say.

Some of the phrases in this book predate Shakespeare but I've included a handful (phrases like 'night owl' or 'dead as doornail') because Shakespeare effortlessly breathed new life into them. Without his intervention such phrases might not have become so widely used, and dare I say, cherished by speakers of the English language today.

Shakespeare's hand in popularizing the 101 phrases contained in this book is, I feel, far more important than the idea of Shakespeare as the originator or inventor of such phrases and idioms.

Shakespeare continues to familiarize us with such language by way of his colossal popularity, and, of course, his superlative examples.

101 Everyday Phrases

 # 01 Everyday Phrase:

All's well that ends well.

MEANING:

If the outcome is good, then difficulties along the way are worth it and/or justifiable.

SHAKESPEARE SOURCE:

All's Well That Ends Well—play title.

STORY EXAMPLE:

The new Prime Minister's victory was hard won. There were many political casualties but that won't matter now. A taste of power and **all's well that ends well** for the incoming resident of Number 10 Downing Street.

CONVERSATION EXAMPLE:

A: I travelled half way around the world to be with my sweetheart.

B: Was it worth it, even though you had to quit your job and say goodbye to your family?

A: Of course it was.

B: Then **all's well that ends well.**

 # 02 Everyday Phrase:

All one to me.

MEANING:

I'm not fussy. I make no distinction between things.

SHAKESPEARE SOURCE:

Troilus and Cressida, Act 1, scene 1.

SHAKESPEARE QUOTE:

PANDARUS: Because she's kin to me, therefore she's not so fair as Helen: an she were not kin to me, she would be as fair on

Friday as Helen is on Sunday. But what care I? I care not an she were a black-a-moor; **'tis all one to me.**

STORY EXAMPLE:

Albert's father told him that if he was going to come home a minute late he might as well be an hour late. It was **all one to him**. Late was late.

CONVERSATION EXAMPLE:

A: What tea do you want?

B: What type do you have?

A: We have green tea, black tea or white tea.

B: I don't care. **It's all one to me**. If it's hot and wet and tastes of tea, I'm happy.

 # 03 Everyday Phrase:

All that glitters[1] is not gold.

MEANING:

Don't be fooled by showy appearances. Just because something looks attractive, it doesn't mean it is.

SHAKESPEARE SOURCE:

Merchant of Venice, Act 2, scene 7.

SHAKESPEARE QUOTE:

MOROCCO: **All that glisters is not gold**—Often have you heard that told.

STORY EXAMPLE:

Consumers should be careful when buying a used car. A seller may have washed and polished the vehicle but remember, **all that glitters is not gold.** Always check the engine and seek the advice of a good mechanic.

CONVERSATION EXAMPLE:

A: Mr. Jones, I think this is the perfect apartment for you.

B: Yes but **all that glitters is not gold**, right?

1 Shakespeare's text uses the word "glisters," a rarely used literary word. Today, its modern equivalent "glitters" has replaced "glisters" in the everyday phrase.

A: I'm sorry? I don't know what you mean.

B: Well, the apartment looks nice but when I checked carefully I found a hole in the bedroom ceiling, bad plumbing in the bathroom and termite damage to the front porch.

 # 04 Everyday Phrase:

As dead as a doornail.[2]

MEANING:

Dead. Broken.

SHAKESPEARE SOURCE:

Henry V1, Part II, Act 4, scene 10.

SHAKESPEARE QUOTE:

JACK CADE: Look on me well: I have eat no meat these five days; yet, come thou and thy five men, and if I do not leave you all as dead as a doornail, I pray God I may never eat grass more.

STORY EXAMPLE:

Clara's computer was broken. She took it to three different repair shops and no one could fix it. She even tried to fix it herself but it was **as dead as a doornail.** She would have to buy a new one.

CONVERSATION EXAMPLE:

A: Is it true that you and Neil broke up last week?

B: Yes it is.

A: Why? I thought you two loved each other.

B: Our love's **as dead as a doornail** and has been for years. We were just too frightened to admit it.

 # 05 Everyday Phrase:

As good luck would have it.

MEANING:

Luckily.

2 This expression is not a Shakespeare original and predates The Bard by a couple hundred years. However, Shakespeare was instrumental in popularizing its use.

Shakespeare source:

The Merry Wives of Windsor, Act 3, scene 5.

Shakespeare quote:

FALSTAFF: You shall hear. **As good luck would have it**, comes in one Mistress Page; gives intelligence of Ford's approach; and, in her invention and Ford's wife's distraction, they conveyed me into a buck-basket.

Story example:

Alan's car broke down on an old desert road miles from the nearest town. Usually, people didn't take the old road but **as good luck would have it** the local sheriff had decided to use the old road that particular afternoon. If Sheriff John Jones hadn't been driving by, Alan might have been stranded there for hours.

Conversation example:

A: I'm so disappointed. I really wanted to go to the concert tonight.

B: Why can't you go?

A: I don't have a ticket. I went online but they're sold out.

B: Well, **as good luck would have it** I have a spare ticket.

 # 06 Everyday Phrase:

As pure as the driven snow.[3]

Meaning:

Utterly pure. Chaste.

Shakespeare source:

Hamlet, Act 3, scene 1.

Shakespeare quote:

HAMLET: If thou dost marry, I'll give thee this plague for thy dowry. Be thou as chaste as ice, **as pure as snow**, thou shalt not escape calumny. Get thee to a nunnery, go. Farewell.

3 "As pure as the *driven* snow" is a modern version of Shakespeare's "As pure as snow." The expression appears in several of his other plays including *Macbeth* and *The Winter's Tale*.

STORY EXAMPLE:

The voters think that Senator Roebuck is **as pure as the driven snow** but if you buy tomorrow's edition of The Inquirer, you'll read a very different story from the senator's former secretary, Nancy Lovelace.

CONVERSATION EXAMPLE:

A: Why does Emily always get the starring role in the school play?

B: Because the director thinks she's **as pure as the driven snow**, that's why.

A: She might look like little Miss Perfect but she certainly doesn't behave like it in rehearsals.

B: If only he knew the truth.

 # 07 Everyday Phrase:

Bated breath.[4]

MEANING:

To hold one's breath and/or to be in a state of anticipation.

SHAKESPEARE SOURCE:

The Merchant of Venice, Act 1, scene 3.

SHAKESPEARE QUOTE:

SHYLOCK: Shall I bend low and in a bondman's key,
With **bated breath** and whispering humbleness, Say this;
'Fair sir, you spit on me on Wednesday last;
You spurn'd me such a day; another time
You call'd me dog; and for these courtesies
I'll lend you thus much moneys'?

STORY EXAMPLE:

Mr. Stein knew that escaping the country with his entire family wouldn't be easy. When the soldiers entered the town, the family waited in the basement with **bated breath** and hoped that a search party wouldn't be sent to search the houses.

---

4 Because the word "bated" is unusual in English, a common written error among native speakers is to use the word "baited," which has the same pronunciation but a different spelling and meaning.

Conversation example:

A: Where's the teacher?

B: In his office drinking coffee.

A: The students are waiting with **bated breath** for their exam grades and he's drinking coffee?

B: Yes. I wish he'd hurry up.

 # 08 Everyday Phrase:

Be all and end all.

Meaning:

The most important moment, detail or event on which everything depends.

Shakespeare source:

Macbeth, Act 1, scene 7.

Shakespeare quote:

MACBETH: If it were done when 'tis done, then 'twere well
It were done quickly. If the assassination
Could trammel up the consequence, and catch
With his surcease success; that but this blow
Might be **the be-all and the end-all** here,
But here, upon this bank and shoal of time,
We'd jump the life to come.

Story example:

No matter how clever, artistic or humorous an advertisement is, the **be all and end all** getting people to buy the product.

Conversation example:

A: Teacher, I'm so disappointed with my grades that I feel like quitting.

B: You're a good student John. I don't think you should quit.

A: But I failed the exam.

B: Failing one exam is not the **be all and end all** of learning English. I'm sure you'll succeed next time.

 # 09 Everyday Phrase:

Bear a charmed life. *(British)*
Lead a charmed life. *(American)*

MEANING:

To have a lucky life.

SHAKESPEARE SOURCE:

Macbeth, Act 5, scene 8.

SHAKESPEARE QUOTE:

MACBETH: Let fall thy blade on vulnerable crests;
I bear a charmed life, which must not yield,
To one of woman born.

STORY EXAMPLE:

She's good-looking, has plenty of money and millions of adoring fans around the world. To many people, Hollywood legend Stella Rockworth **bears a charmed life** that is full of fun and happiness.

CONVERSATION EXAMPLE:

A: Harry must have a great job if he's sailing around the world in a new yacht.

B: He doesn't have a job! In fact, he retired last month.

A: Retired? But he's only fifty years old!

B: Well, you know Harry. He **bears a charmed life** and always will.

 # 10 Everyday Phrase:

Brave new world.[5]

MEANING:

A world full of promise and hope. A futuristic world full of technological advances.

SHAKESPEARE SOURCE:

Tempest, Act 5, scene 1.

5 Brave New World is also the title of a novel by Aldous Huxley. Written in 1931, Brave New World is considered one of the finest novels of the 20th century.

Shakespeare quote:

MIRANDA: O wonder!
How many goodly creatures are there here!
How beauteous mankind is! **O brave new world**,
That has such people in't.

Story example:

The new coach made radical changes to the team and introduced a computer assisted training program to target each player's individual strengths and weaknesses. The cutting-edge technology is part of a **brave new world** for the national squad, and while it won't guarantee them a place in the final, it might just improve their chances.

Conversation example:

A: My new cell phone can do everything?

B: Can it give you a hug or tell you it loves you?

A: No but it can program my TV, start the dishwasher, and turn on the lights.

B: What a **brave new world** we live in.

Quick Quiz 1

Read the sentences below and decide whether the definitions are correct or not. Circle TRUE or FALSE accordingly. Answers to the *Quick Quizzes* can be found at the back of the book.

1. A person with **bated breath** has a bad smell in their mouth.	TRUE / FALSE
2. **As dead as a doornail** means almost dead.	TRUE / FALSE
3. To **bear a charmed life** means to have great luck and success.	TRUE / FALSE
4. The most important detail on which everything depends is known as the **be all and end all.**	TRUE / FALSE
5. **All that glitters is not gold** means taking part is just as important as winning	TRUE / FALSE
6. **Brave new world** refers to modern cities or new countries.	TRUE / FALSE
7. **As pure as the driven snow** means that driving in snow can be an exciting experience.	TRUE / FALSE
8. **As good luck would have it** means fortunately.	TRUE / FALSE
9. **All one to me** means that I am unaffected or simply don't care about differences between things.	TRUE / FALSE
10. **All's well that ends well** means the result is worth the effort.	TRUE / FALSE

 # 11 Everyday Phrase:

Beggars all description. *(British)*

Meaning:

Impossible to describe.

Shakespeare source:

Antony and Cleopatra, Act 2, scene 2.

Shakespeare quote:

ENOBARBUS: For her own person,

It **beggar'd all description**. She did lie
In her pavilion, cloth-of-gold, of tissue,
O'erpicturing that Venus where we see
The fancy out-work nature.

Story example:

The banquet was so sumptuous, the cuisine so fine and the guests so entertaining that it **beggared all description**. You simply had to be there to appreciate the wonder of the occasion.

Conversation example:

A: Can you give me some advice, Jim? I want to invest some money.

B: Don't put it in the bank. The interest rates are too low these days.

A: The banks **beggar all description**, don't they!

B: They sure do. They're happy to take our money but not willing to give a decent return.

 # 12 Everyday Phrase:

Break the ice.

Meaning:

To overcome shyness, embarrassment or social awkwardness within a group or gathering, usually by way of friendly and relaxed conversation.

Shakespeare source:

Taming of the Shrew, Act 1, scene 2.

SHAKESPEARE QUOTE:

TRANIO: *(As LUCENTIO)* If it be so, sir, that you are the man
Must stead us all, and me amongst the rest,
And if you **break the ice** and do this feat,
Achieve the elder, set the younger free
For our access, whose hap shall be to have her
Will not so graceless be to be ingrate.

STORY EXAMPLE:

John was very nervous when he met his girlfriend's parents for the first time. Luckily, his girlfriend's dad **broke the ice** by telling John about his recent trip to Hawaii.

CONVERSATION EXAMPLE:

A: How was your first day on the new job?

B: Great. I was nervous but my supervisor **broke the ice** by telling a few jokes when he introduced me to my coworkers.

A: That's good news. I think you're going to be very happy there.

 # 13 Everyday Phrase:

Brevity is the soul of wit.

MEANING:

Humor and jokes work best when short.

SHAKESPEARE SOURCE:

Hamlet, Act 2, scene 2.

SHAKESPEARE QUOTE:

POLONIUS: …since **brevity is the soul** of wit,
And tediousness the limbs and outward flourishes,
I will be brief: your noble son is mad.

STORY EXAMPLE:

If **brevity is the soul of wit**, then many stand-up comedians have a hard job. Short jokes means a thirty minute routine will contain hundreds of one-liners.

CONVERSATION EXAMPLE:

A: What do you call a blind reindeer?

B: No idea *(No eye deer).*

A: That's funny.

B: That's because **brevity is the soul of wit.**

 # 14 Everyday Phrase:

Cold comfort.

MEANING:

Of little or no sympathy, help or consolation.

SHAKESPEARE SOURCE:

The Taming of the Shrew, Act 4, scene 1.

SHAKESPEARE QUOTE:

GRUMIO: But wilt thou make a fire, or shall I complain on thee to our mistress, whose hand, she being now at hand, thou shalt soon feel, to thy **cold comfort**, for being slow in thy hot office?

STORY EXAMPLE:

Phillip was devastated that he wouldn't play in the final match. He would still receive a finalist's medal but that was **cold comfort** to a player who loved his team and wanted to play at all costs.

CONVERSATION EXAMPLE:

A: Darling, my new handbag was a great deal and I was so lucky because it was the last one.

A: How much did it cost sweetheart?

B: Only four hundred dollars! It was eight hundred originally. I saved fifty percent!

A: That's **cold comfort** to me and **cold comfort** to my poor bank balance.

 # 15 Everyday Phrase:

Come full circle.

MEANING:

To return to a starting point in life, philosophy, action etc.

SHAKESPEARE SOURCE:

King Lear, Act 5, scene 3.

SHAKESPEARE QUOTE:

EDMUND: Thou hast spoken right, 'tis true;
The wheel is **come full circle**: I am here.

STORY EXAMPLE:

Mr. Forsyth sold his 1972 Mustang years ago but things **came full circle** when his youngest son bought exactly the same car at an auto auction last year.

CONVERSATION EXAMPLE:

A: I went to Vegas with ten dollars and I came home with ten dollars.

B: So you didn't win any money gambling?

A: Yes, I won ten thousand dollars but then I lost it all.

B: Things **came full circle** in the end. You're lucky you still have your ten dollars.

 # 16 Everyday Phrase:

Come what come may.

MEANING:

No matter what may occur. In spite of everything.

SHAKESPEARE SOURCE:

Macbeth, Act 1, scene 3.

SHAKESPEARE QUOTE:

MACBETH: **Come what come may,**
Time and the hour runs through the roughest day.

STORY EXAMPLE:

Alistair had trained long and hard for the marathon and even though he had injured his ankle the week before the race, **come what come may**, he was determined to cross the finishing line.

CONVERSATION EXAMPLE:

A: It's a shame you can't come home on Thanksgiving. Everyone will miss you.

B: Don't worry. I'll be there.

A: I thought you had to work.

B: I do but **come what come may** I'll find a way to get home.

 # 17 Everyday Phrase:

(The course of) true love never does/did run smooth.

Meaning:

Love is difficult sometimes.

Shakespeare source:

A Midsummer Night's Dream, Act 1, scene 1.

Shakespeare quote:

LYSANDER: Ay me! For aught that I could ever read,
Could ever hear by tale or history,
The course of true love never did run smooth.

Story example:

After her seventh marriage, Dina was convinced she had finally found her perfect match but Dina tried not to get too excited. History had taught her that the course of **true love never did run smooth.**

Conversation example:

A: I had a terrible argument with my husband last night.

B: I'm sorry to hear that.

A: We've been happily married for years but we still fight sometimes.

B: That's life. **True loves never does run smooth.**

 # 18 Everyday Phrase:

Cruel to be kind.

Meaning:

To cause a person suffering for their own good.

Shakespeare source:

Hamlet, Act 3, scene 4.

Shakespeare quote:

HAMLET: I will bestow him and will answer well
The death I gave him. So, again, good night.
I must be **cruel only to be kind.**
Thus bad begins and worse remains behind.

Story example:

The teacher made the students study very hard before the exam. He even gave them extra homework. They weren't very happy but he was being **cruel to be kind** and knew the extra work would help them succeed.

Conversation example:

A: Why did you eat my chocolate ice-cream?

B: I was being **cruel to be kind**.

A: What do you mean?

B: You told me you were on a diet so I thought I'd help you.

 # 19 Everyday Phrase:

Dash to pieces.[6] *(British)*
Smash to smithereens. *(American and British)*

Meaning:

To destroy.

Shakespeare source:

The Tempest, Act 1, scene 2.

Shakespeare quote:

MIRANDA: Oh, I have suffered
With those that I saw suffer. A brave vessel
Who had, no doubt, some noble creature in her
Dashed all to pieces. Oh, the cry did knock
Against my very heart! Poor souls, they perished.

Story example:

Lee's hopes were **dashed to pieces** when he found out Jennifer was going to the prom with someone else. He really regrets not asking her sooner.

Conversation example:

A: My three-year-old son had a terrible tantrum this morning.

6 The phrase "dash to pieces" makes several appearances in the Shakespeare canon: *Henry IV - Part II, Julius Caesar,* and *Richard III*, all of which were written before Shakespeare had penned The Tempest (which I cite here because of *Miranda's* line despairing over the shipwreck she has just witnessed.

B: What happened?

A: I was feeding him some rice and peas when he picked up the plate and **dashed it to pieces** on the floor.

B: Oh dear!

 # 20 Everyday Phrase:

Devil incarnate.

Meaning:

Evil personified.

Shakespeare source:

Henry V, Act 2, scene 3.

Shakespeare quote:

BOY: Yes, that a' did; and said they (women) were **devils incarnate.**

Story example:

Most of the striking workers outside the factory believe the company director is the **devil incarnate,** a man wholly responsible for the current unrest.

Conversation example:

A: You look terrible. What's wrong?

B: My wife just called and said my mother-in-law is coming to stay for three weeks.

A: Is she really that bad?

B: She's the **devil incarnate** and I don't know how I'm going to survive.

Quick Quiz 2

Decide which idiom or phrase best fits the blank spaces in the sentences below.

1. It's important to _________________________ and make newcomers feel welcome.
2. The 150ft sculpture has to be seen to be appreciated. It _________________________.
3. His first job was at the New York office. Now, many years later he is returning as manager. He really feels his life has _________________________.
4. I make you practice every day because sometimes a good teacher has to be _________________________.
5. I'm determined and know _________________________ I will succeed.
6. When telling a joke, keep it short and remember that _________________________.
7. When Jane rejected John's marriage proposal his hopes were _________________________.
8. The prisoner's death sentence was commuted to life in prison but that was _________________________ to a man who would never be free again.
9. When Jan and Dave broke up last week they both learned a painful lesson of the heart:_______________________.
10. After Mrs. Simpson's new puppy attacked the neighbor's cat, ate Mr. Simpson's left slipper and used her living room sofa as a doggy bathroom she was convinced the animal was the _________________________.

#21 Everyday Phrase:

A dish fit for the gods.

Meaning:

An extremely good meal, dish.

Shakespeare source:

Julius Caesar, Act 2, scene 1.

Shakespeare quote:

BRUTUS: Let's be sacrificers, but not butchers, Caius.
. . . And, gentle friends,
Let's kill him boldly, but not wrathfully;
Let's carve him as a **dish fit for the gods,**
Not hew him as a carcass fit for hounds.

Story example:

Pierre's dinner guests congratulated him on his wonderful cooking. Everyone agreed that the duck in Armagnac sauce had been a **dish fit for the gods**.

Conversation example:

A: What are you eating?

B: Peanut butter and cucumber sandwiches.

A: That's sounds disgusting!

B: You should try it. It's a **dish fit for the gods.**

 # 22 Everyday Phrase:

Done to death.

Meaning:

Something so often repeated that it loses its appeal, freshness or enjoyment.

Shakespeare source:

Much Ado About Nothing, Act 5, scene 3.

Shakespeare quote:

CLAUDIO: **Done to death** by slanderous tongue
Was the Hero that here lies.

STORY EXAMPLE:

Many high school drama departments don't seem to know that Shakespeare wrote more than two plays. This might explain why *A Midsummer Night's Dream* and *Romeo and Juliet* are **done to death** year after year.

CONVERSATION EXAMPLE:

A: Do you come here often?

B: That chat up line has been **done to death**. Have you got another?

A: Sure. If this bar's a meat market, you must be the prime rib.

B: Okay, you can leave now.

 # 23 Everyday Phrase:

Eaten out of house and home.

MEANING:

To have one's entire supply of food greatly reduced, often by a guest or guests.

SHAKESPEARE SOURCE:

Henry IV, Part II, Act 2, scene 1.

SHAKESPEARE QUOTE:

MISTRESS QUICKLY: He hath **eaten me out of house and home**; he hath put all my substance into that fat belly of his: but I will have some of it out again, or I will ride thee o' nights like the mare.

STORY EXAMPLE:

Barbara's son was home from college. He brought a bag of dirty washing, a new girlfriend and spent the whole weekend **eating her out of house and home.** Barbara didn't care. She was happy to have her baby home again.

CONVERSATION EXAMPLE:

A: Shall I invite Uncle Bert to stay during the holidays?

B: That depends on how long he plans to stay.

A: He can stay as long as he likes!

B: Well, I'm not buying all the food. Last time he stayed for a month and **ate us out of house and home.**

 # 24 Everyday Phrase:

Elbow room.

Meaning:

Sufficient or adequate space or scope.

Shakespeare source:

King John, Act 5, scene 7.

Shakespeare quote:

KING JOHN: Ay, marry, now my soul hath **elbow-room**; It would not out at windows nor at doors.

Story example:

Jerry doesn't like his new car. It's economical and gets great gas mileage but there just isn't enough **elbow room** for Jerry, his wife and their nine children.

Conversation example:

A: I love Ms. Bertram's music class.

B: So do I. She always explains things clearly.

A: And she gives us plenty of **elbow room** to try new things.

B: I agree. She's the best music teacher I've ever had.

 # 25 Everyday Phrase:

Eyesore.

Meaning:

Something ugly or unsightly such as a derelict building.

Shakespeare source:

The Rape of Lucrece, Line 205.

Shakespeare quote:

'Yea, though I die, the scandal will survive,
And be an **eye-sore** in my golden coat…

Story example:

Once described as an 'architectural wonder,' by city authorities, today, many residents consider Main Library the city's **eyesore.**

CONVERSATION EXAMPLE:

A: Someone has sprayed graffiti over the entire neighborhood.

B: Who would do such a thing?

A: I don't know but I'm going to help clean up the **eyesore.**

B: Wait for me, I'll grab my coat.

 # 26 Everyday Phrase:

Faint-hearted.

MEANING:

Lacking conviction or courage.

SHAKESPEARE SOURCE:

Henry VI, Part III, Act 1, scene 1.

SHAKESPEARE QUOTE:

WESTMORELAND: Farewell, **faint-hearted** and degenerate king, In whose cold blood no spark of honour bides.

STORY EXAMPLE:

Andy's best man had arranged a stag-night of drinking, singing and dancing. The evening's entertainment included a visit to Ma Rogers, one of the finest whisky bars in the city. With over three hundred whiskies to choose from it clearly wasn't going to be a night for the **faint-hearted** (or the weak-livered).

CONVERSATION EXAMPLE:

A: Do you want to go to the movies tonight?

B: Sure. What's on?

A: A new horror movie called, *ESL Teacher from Hell!!!*

B: Will it be scary?

A: Let's just say, it's not for the **faint-hearted.**

B: Well, it can't be scarier than studying the passive voice, surely?!

 # 27 Everyday Phrase:

Fair play.

MEANING:

To observe the correct rules and follow an established code of decency and fairness.

Shakespeare source:

The Tempest, Act 5, scene 1.

Shakespeare quote:

MIRANDA: Yes, for a score of kingdoms you should wrangle,
And I would call it, **fair play.**

Story example:

During the soccer match an opposition player fell and broke his leg. Jenkins showed great maturity and a sense of **fair play** by giving up his attack on goal and going immediately to the injured player's assistance.

Conversation example:

A: Do you think I should tell Matthew that I plan to ask Jennifer out on a date?

B: No I don't. Why should you tell Matthew?

A: Well, he likes Jennifer too.

B: There's no **fair play** in love.

A: I just hope he hasn't asked her out already.

 # 28 Everyday Phrase:

Fancy-free.

Meaning:

Carefree and without commitments.

Shakespeare source:

A Midsummer Night's Dream, Act 2, scene 1.

Shakespeare quote:

OBERON: But I might see young Cupid's fiery shaft
Quenched in the chaste beams of the watery moon,
And the imperial votaress passed on,
In maiden meditation, **fancy-free.**

Story example:

Mrs. Eldridge wished her eldest son Edward would grow up, get married and provide her with some grandchildren. He was almost forty and still running around town chasing girls half his age like a **fancy-free** Don Juan without a care in the world.

CONVERSATION EXAMPLE:

A: Why don't you give me a call this evening and we'll do something.

B: What?

A: I don't know. I'm **fancy-free** so let's just go wherever the night takes us.

B: Sounds great.

 # 29 Everyday Phrase:

Fight fire with fire.[7]

MEANING:

Respond to an attack with equal ferocity and aggression.

SHAKESPEARE SOURCE:

King John, Act 5, scene 1.

SHAKESPEARE QUOTE:

BASTARD: Be great in act, as you have been in thought;
Let not the world see fear and sad distrust
Govern the motion of a kingly eye:
Be stirring as the time; **be fire with fire**;
Threaten the threatener and outface the brow
Of bragging horror.

STORY EXAMPLE:

The government announced that it would never negotiate with terrorists and that the preferred response was to **fight fire with fire.**

CONVERSATION EXAMPLE:

A: Is it true that Jim has cancer?

B: Yes and that's why he has decided to take a course of chemotherapy.

A: But isn't chemotherapy dangerous?

B: Yes but he needs to **fight fire with fire** if he's going to beat this disease.

---

7 Shakespeare's "*be fire with fire*" captures much the same meaning as "*fight fire with fire*" and is an early precursor of the phrase that originated amongst firefighters much later than Shakespeare's time.

 # 30 Everyday Phrase:

A fool's paradise.

Meaning:

A state of happiness that is based on false belief or hopes.

Shakespeare source:

Romeo & Juliet, Act 2 scene 4.

Shakespeare quote:

NURSE: Pray you, sir, a word. And as I told you, my young lady bid me inquire you out. What she bade me say, I will keep to myself. But first let me tell ye, if ye should lead her into a **fool's paradise**, as they say, it were a very gross kind of behavior, as they say.

Story example:

Anyone who thinks man's continued addiction to fossil fuels is not a threat to human existence is living in a **fool's paradise.**

Conversation example:

A: Tomorrow, I'm going to quit smoking.

B: Why don't you start right now?

A: I've already cut down and I'm only smoking low tar cigarettes now.

B: If you think low tar cigarettes are healthy, you're in a **fool's paradise.**

Quick Quiz 3

What idioms or phrases best match the descriptions below.

1. Plenty of space for movement.
2. An extremely good meal.
3. An unsightly building.
4. Carefree.
5. Someone who lacks conviction.
6. Lacking originality. Often repeated.
7. To defend yourself by attacking your opponent with equal force.
8. Good sportsmanship.
9. A false sense of contentment.
10. To have one's food supply depleted by a guest or visitor.

 # 31 Everyday Phrase:

Foregone conclusion.

Meaning:

An outcome that is obvious or inevitable.

Shakespeare source:

Othello, Act 3, scene 3

Shakespeare quote:

IAGO: In sleep I heard him say "Sweet Desdemona,
Let us be wary, let us hide our loves."

OTHELLO: Oh, monstrous! Monstrous!

IAGO: Nay, this was but his dream.

OTHELLO: But this denoted a **foregone conclusion**.

Story example:

As soon as he saw the car Jim knew that buying it was a **foregone conclusion**. The price was good, the engine and body were in perfect condition and it only had five-hundred miles on the clock.

Conversation example:

A: I think Jack and Jane make a great couple.

B: You're right. They're perfect for each other.

A: Do you think they'll get married?

B: It's a **foregone conclusion**.

 # 32 Everyday Phrase:

For ever and a day.

Meaning:

For a very, very long time.

Shakespeare source:

As You Like It, Act 4, scene 1.

Shakespeare quote:

ROSALIND: Now tell me how long you would have her after you have possessed her.

ORLANDO: **For ever and a day.**

STORY EXAMPLE:

Mr. Kim wondered if he would ever speak English fluently. Sometimes, he thought speaking English was easy and other times he thought it would take **forever and day** to reach his goal.

CONVERSATION EXAMPLE:

A: Did you and your wife enjoy the meal last night?

B: No we didn't and we are never going back to that terrible restaurant again.

A: I'm sorry to hear that. What was the problem?

B: We had to wait **forever and a day** to get served and when the food finally came it was cold!

A: That's too bad. I hope you complained.

 # 33 Everyday Phrase:

Foul play.

MEANING:

Underhand, dishonest or criminal behavior.

SHAKESPEARE SOURCE:

Hamlet, Act 1, scene 2.

SHAKESPEARE QUOTE:

HAMLET: My father's spirit in arms! all is not well;
I doubt some **foul play**: would the night were come!

STORY EXAMPLE:

Everyone in the village believed that Mrs. Kendall had died in a tragic accident but Detective Owen was not so sure. He suspected **foul play** and wanted to know why Mrs. Kendall's fifth husband, George, had changed his story about his whereabouts on the night of her death.

CONVERSATION EXAMPLE:

A: Every student had exactly the same answers on the test.

B: How is that possible? They must have cheated.

A: That's what Principal James thinks. He suspects **foul play.**

 # 34 Everyday Phrase:

The game is up.

Meaning:

A deception is uncovered.

Shakespeare source:

Cymbeline, Act 3, scene 3.

Shakespeare quote:

BELARIUS: Thou wast their nurse; they took thee for their mother,
And every day do honour to her grave:
Myself, Belarius, that am Morgan call'd,
They take for natural father. **The game is up**.

Story example:

Unable to hide his enormous stock market losses, the rogue trader knew **the game was up**. He packed a suitcase, wrote himself a company check for three million dollars and disappeared.

Conversation example:

A: You ate my chocolate cake, didn't you?

B: No, I didn't.

A: I know you're lying because you have chocolate on your face and crumbs all over your sweater.

B: Okay, okay, **the game is up**, I admit it. I'm a secret 'chocoholic.'

 # 35 Everyday Phrase:

(To) Gild the lily.[8]

Meaning:

To embellish.

Shakespeare source:

King John, Act 4, scene 2.

Shakespeare quote:

SALISBURY: To guard a title that was rich before,

8 The phrase *"To gild the lily"* is a bastardized version of the original "*to gild refined gold, to paint the lily*," and demonstrates what can happen when enough people misquote a phrase for long enough: it becomes the accepted version.

To **gild refined gold, to paint the lily**,
To throw a perfume on the violet,
To smooth the ice, or add another hue
Unto the rainbow, or with taper-light
To seek the beauteous eye of heaven to garnish,
Is wasteful and ridiculous excess.

Story example:

Children don't need embellishment but try telling that to moms at this year's National Victory Pageant who insist on **gilding the lily** with wildly expensive gowns and excessive amounts of make-up.

Conversation example:

A: What do you think of my new outfit?

B: I'd lose the tiara. Its **gilding the lily**, don't you think?

A: What wrong with it?

B: Nothing but you're going on a dinner date not meeting the Queen of England.

 # 36 Everyday Phrase:

Good riddance.

Meaning:

An exclamation of contentment at being rid of something or someone.

Shakespeare source:

Troilus and Cressida, Act 2, scene 1.

Shakespeare quote:

THERSITES: I will see you hang'd like clatpoles ere I come any more to your tents. I will keep where there is wit stirring, and leave thefaction of fools. *[Exit]*

PATROCLUS: A **good riddance**.

Story example:

Julie was *Teen Love Joy*'s biggest fan until she heard that lead singer Gordon Sparkles was getting engaged. The day she found out, Julie said **good riddance** to 'TLJ.' She'd find another pop star to fall in love with, one that wouldn't break her heart.

Conversation example:

A: I heard that you're moving to Downtown.

B: Yes, I found a great apartment near my office.

A: Won't you miss living in the suburbs?

B: **Good riddance** to the suburbs. I'm ready for some fun in the city.

 # 37 Everyday Phrase:

Green-eyed monster.

Meaning:

Jealousy.

Shakespeare source:

Othello, Act 3, scene 3.

Shakespeare quote:

IAGO: O, beware, my lord, of jealousy;
It is the **green-ey'd monster**, which doth mock
The meat it feeds on.

Story example:

Teddy had always been a very jealous husband. If his wife even looked at another man the **green-eyed monster** would take hold of him and Teddy would sulk for days without speaking a word to his wife.

Conversation example:

A: Norris is so handsome that I don't understand why he hasn't got a girlfriend?

B: Because the **green-eyed monster** makes him so unhappy he decided to quit dating all together.

A: Poor Norris. He really should talk to a counselor.

 # 38 Everyday Phrase:

Halcyon days.

Meaning:

Expression often used nostalgically that refers to carefree, happy days of youth.

Shakespeare source:

Henry VI, Part I, Act 1, scene 2.

Shakespeare quote:

JOAN LA PUCELLE: Assign'd am I to be the English scourge. This night the siege assuredly I'll raise:Expect Saint Martin's summer, **halcyon days**, Since I have entered into these wars.

Story example:

Edward and Louise have become good friends since Edward moved to the nursing home a few months ago. He is ninety-four and she is ninety-three. They sit around the fireplace most days, holding hands and talking long into the night about the **halcyon days** of their youth.

Conversation example:

A: Do you remember the long summers we used to spend on the Isle of Mull?

B: Of course I do.

A: We had such fun, playing on the beach, making sandcastles, splashing in the sea.

B: I'll never forget **halcyon days** like those. They were magical times.

 # 39 Everyday Phrase:

(To one's) heart's content.

Meaning:

To do something for as long as one so wishes or desires.

Shakespeare source:

The Merchant of Venice, Act 3, scene 4.

Shakespeare quote:

JESSICA: I wish your ladyship all **heart's content.**

PORTIA: I thank you for your wish, and am well pleased

To wish it back on you. Fare you well, Jessica.

Story example:

Billy's mother and father were going to be out of town for the whole weekend, which meant Jimmy could turn up the volume on the stereo and play his favorite rock 'n' roll tunes **to his heart's content.**

Conversation example:

A: I've just booked my summer vacation and I can't wait.

B: Where are you going?

A: I'm going on an all-inclusive Caribbean cruise.

B: Wow! You'll be able to go sightseeing, eat, drink and dance **to your heart's content.**

 # 40 Everyday Phrase:

High time.

Meaning:

The time to act is due or overdue.

Shakespeare source:

The Comedy of Errors, Act 3, scene 2.

Shakespeare quote:

ANTIPHOLUS OF SYRACUSE: There's none but witches do inhabit here; And therefore 'tis **high time** that I were hence.

Story example:

Everyone agreed it was **high time** Adam went to see a doctor. He had been feeling ill for months but kept putting off a visit to the clinic.

Conversation example:

A: Mum, have you seen my shirt?

B: No I haven't.

A: I can't find it anywhere. Where could it be?

B: It's **high time** you stopped asking silly questions and started thinking for yourself.

Quick Quiz 4

Circle the incorrect word in each phrase and write the correct phrase in the space provided.

1. The game is down. ____________________.
2. Four play. ____________________.
3. Bad riddance. ____________________.
4. Blue-eyed monster. ____________________.
5. Halcyon years. ____________________.
6. Tall time. ____________________.
7. Glide the lily. ____________________.
8. Forgotten conclusion. ____________________.
9. For Trevor and a day. ____________________.
10. To my heart's context. ____________________.

 # 41 Everyday Phrase:

Hot-blooded.

Meaning:

Having a lusty, passionate or short-tempered nature.

Shakespeare source:

The Merry Wives Of Windsor, Act 5, scene 5.

Shakespeare quote:

FALSTAFF: The Windsor bell hath struck twelve; the minute draws on. Now, the **hot-blooded** gods assist me!

Story example:

Xavier was a brilliant scholar and **hot-blooded** young man whose antics were legendary throughout the college. His fellow students joked that his girlfriends were so numerous that the entrance to his bedroom should be replaced with a revolving door.

Conversation example:

A: Have you met Natalie's new boyfriend yet?

B: No but I heard he's more of a horny old goat than a **hot-blooded** young buck.

A: Yes, he's thirty years her senior. What do you think she sees in him?

B: His wallet.

 # 42 Everyday Phrase:

Improbable fiction.

Meaning:

An unlikely story or account.

Shakespeare source:

Twelfth Night, Act 3, scene 4.

Shakespeare quote:

FABIAN: If this were played upon a stage now, I could condemn it as an **improbable fiction.**

STORY EXAMPLE:

The story of the team's success sounds like an **improbable fiction** but judging by their meteoric rise from the bottom of the league to the top, it appears that miracles really are possible.

CONVERSATION EXAMPLE:

A: Where's your homework Smithers?

B: The dog ate it, sir.

A: That's an **improbable fiction**. Bring it tomorrow or you'll be in detention for the rest of the week.

B: Yes, sir.

 # 43 Everyday Phrase:

In a pickle.

MEANING:

To be in a difficult or bewildering situation.

SHAKESPEARE SOURCE:

The Tempest, Act 5, scene 1.

SHAKESPEARE QUOTE:

TRINCULO: I have been **in such a pickle** since I
saw you last that, I fear me, will never out of
my bones: I shall not fear fly-blowing.

STORY EXAMPLE:

Martha failed her driving test because she was **in a pickle** and didn't focus. The traffic was bad and the weather was stormy. And when the examiner told her to turn left, she turned right and drove straight into a tree.

CONVERSATION EXAMPLE:

A: I feel so sorry for Jim. After the accident he lost his job, his wife and his house.

B: That's terrible! It sounds like he's **in a real pickle**! We should call him.

A: That's a great idea but his phone was cut off too.

B: Wow! He really is **in a pickle**.

A: Let's go round and see him instead.

 # 44 Everyday Phrase:

In my heart of hearts.

MEANING:

One's truest and innermost feelings.

SHAKESPEARE SOURCE:

Hamlet, Act 3, scene 2.

SHAKESPEARE QUOTE:

HAMLET: . . . Give me that man
That is not passion's slave, and I will wear him
In my heart's core, ay, **in my heart of hearts**,
As I do thee.

STORY EXAMPLE:

When Fran moved to London her parents worried about her being so far from home, but **in her heart of hearts** Fran always knew that London was the city for her.

CONVERSATION EXAMPLE:

A: Mom, why did you marry Dad?

B: I sometimes ask myself that same question, honey, but **in my heart of hearts,** I knew the moment I met him that your father was the right man for me.

 # 45 Everyday Phrase:

In my mind's eye.

MEANING:

Refers to the human ability to visualize, picture or see images with one's mind.

SHAKESPEARE SOURCE:

Hamlet, Act 1, scene 2.

SHAKESPEARE QUOTE:

HAMLET: My father!—methinks I see my father.

HORATIO: Where, my lord?

HAMLET: **In my mind's eye**, Horatio.

STORY EXAMPLE:

Today's athletes not only train physically for big competitions but also prepare mentally. Picturing future success in **the mind's eye** can help give sportsmen and women greater focus and determination.

CONVERSATION EXAMPLE:

A: Do you remember the wonderful vacation we had in Scotland?

B: Of course I do. I'll never forget it.

A: We stayed in that little cottage near the beach.

B: The sand was so white and the sea so blue.

A: I can picture it so clearly **in my mind's eye.** We really should go back one day.

B: We will.

 # 46 Everyday Phrase:

In stitches.

MEANING:

To laugh hysterically/uncontrollably.

SHAKESPEARE SOURCE:

Twelfth Night, Act 3, scene 2.

SHAKESPEARE QUOTE:

MARIA: If you desire the spleen, and will laugh yourself **into stitches**, follow me.

STORY EXAMPLE:

Rosie was **in stitches** when she saw the latest episode of Crudmore Farm. It's her favorite program, she's never missed it and thinks the characters and storylines are hilarious.

CONVERSATION EXAMPLE:

A: I went to see a stand-up comedian performing at the Vortex Theatre last night?

B: Was he funny?

A: Yes he was. He had me **in stitches** all night.

 # 47 Everyday Phrase:

It's Greek to me.

Meaning:

Used to express a lack of understanding or knowledge.

Shakespeare source:

Julius Caesar, Act 1, scene 2.

Shakespeare quote:

CASCA: But those that understood him smiled at one another and shook their heads. But, for mine own part, it was **Greek to me.**

Story example:

Megan couldn't help her daughter with her math homework because it **was Greek to her**. She had never understood algebra and feared she never would.

Conversation example:

A: Did you fix your car?

B: No. I read the owner's manual but **it's all Greek to me**. I guess I'll have to take it to a mechanic.

A: Sounds expensive.

 # 48 Everyday Phrase:

It smells to heaven.[9]

Meaning:

To have a bad smell. Expresses incredulity.

Shakespeare source:

Hamlet, Act 3, scene 3.

Shakespeare quote:

CLAUDIUS: Oh, my offence is rank. **It smells to heaven**.

Story example:

Police suspect that Mr. Browne may have burned down his store to receive the large insurance payout. Detectives are

9 "Stinks to heaven" has become a popular alternative to the original phrase.

working hard to uncover the truth. Even Mr. Browne's own business partners say that his story about what happened on the night of the fire **smells to heaven.**

CONVERSATION EXAMPLE:

A: I found a dead rat in the basement this morning.

B: That's disgusting.

A: Yes and **it smelled to heaven** too.

 # 49 Everyday Phrase:

Kill with kindness.

MEANING:

To be overly kind (often with an ulterior motive in mind).

SHAKESPEARE SOURCE:

Taming of the Shrew, Act 4, scene 1.

SHAKESPEARE QUOTE:

PETRUCHIO: And if s he chance to nod I'll rail and brawl,
And with the clamor keep her still awake.
This is a way to **kill a wife with kindness,**
And thus I'll curb her mad and headstrong humor.

STORY EXAMPLE:

Ever since Mildred won the lottery last week her boyfriend Gerald has been **killing her with kindness**. Of course, she's flattered by all the attention, but she's never seen this side of him before. He cleaned her apartment, washed her car, and last night appeared outside her bedroom window strumming a guitar with a flower between his teeth.

CONVERSATION EXAMPLE:

A: I really hope the boss gives me time off for my family reunion next month.

B: Ah, so that's why you've been **killing him with kindness** all week.

A: I don't know what you're talking about.

B: Well, you took him coffee and doughnuts every morning, offered to work overtime at the weekends, and even said you'd pick up his shirts from the dry cleaners.

50 EVERYDAY PHRASE:

Knock, knock! Who's there?[10]

MEANING:

A popular joke format with a question and answer structure.

SHAKESPEARE SOURCE:

Macbeth, Act 2, scene 3.

SHAKESPEARE QUOTE:

PORTER: **Knock, knock, knock! Who's there,** i' th' name of Beelzebub?

STORY EXAMPLE:

At this stage of the child's psychological development they have become far more social. They love to laugh and enjoy sharing jokes and riddles. By the age of 6-7 years old the classic, **"Knock, knock! Who's there?"** jokes we remember from our own childhood are real crowd pleaser.

CONVERSATION EXAMPLE:

A: **Knock, knock!**

B: **Who's there?**

A: Ice cream.

B: "Ice cream" who?

B: Ice cream if you don't open this door!

10 The Porter is one of Shakespeare most famous comic roles but the tradition of telling "knock, knock, who's there" jokes didn't originate until the 20th century.

Quick Quiz 5

Choose the correct answers from the multiple choice list below:

1. To laugh heartily is to be . . .

a) in sutures | b) in session
c) in stitches | d) in solids

2. If you are hot-blooded, you might . . .

a) be passionate | b) like spicy food
c) be sick | d) sunbathe a lot

3. If someone is in a pickle they are . . .

a) dead | b) stuck in traffic
c) embarrassed | d) having difficulty

4. It's Greek to me means . . .

a) I'm sure | b) it's romantic
c) I don't understand | d) I love this music

5. An improbable fiction is . . .

a) a great novel | b) a bad novel
c) an unlikely story | d) a short story

6. The second line of a 'knock knock' joke is always . . .

a) How's that? | b) He's here
c) Who me? | d) Who's there?

7.If something smells to heaven it . . .

a) smells wonderful | b) smells terrible
c) doesn't smell | d) looks nice

8.To kill someone with kindness means to . . .

a) kill someone humanely | b) be too kind
c) kiss someone | d) tell someone you like them

9. In my heart of hearts means . . .

a) I am in love
b) I am broken hearted.
c) my true feelings
d) I have heart problems

10.My mind's eye is . . .

a) used to visualize things
b) a sign of bad eyesight
c) the center of the brain
d) a good memory

51 Everyday Phrase:

The lady doth protest too much, methinks.

MEANING:

A strong denial or objection that does not seem truthful. The forcefulness of such a denial may lead us to doubt the credibility of the speaker's words.

SHAKESPEARE SOURCE:

Hamlet, Act 3, scene 2.

SHAKESPEARE QUOTE:

HAMLET: Madam, how like you this play?

GERTRUDE: **The lady doth protest too much, methinks.**

STORY EXAMPLE:

Irene made such a fuss over the disappearance of her sister's favorite hat that everyone could see **the lady had protested too much**. She was clearly guilty.

CONVERSATION EXAMPLE:

A: I don't find Tom Carter attractive and I never have.

B: Okay.

A: You may have heard the rumors about Tom and me but they're not true.

B: Sure.

A: I just want to let you know that I didn't meet him in the park yesterday, we didn't hold hands and we certainly didn't kiss each other.

B: **The lady doth protest too much methinks**.

52 Everyday Phrase:

Laid on with a trowel. *(British)*
Laid on with a shovel. *(American)*

MEANING:

To exaggerate, overstate or overdo.

SHAKESPEARE SOURCE:

As You Like It, Act 1, scene 2.

Shakespeare quote:

CELIA: Well said. That **was laid on with a trowel.**

Story example:

When the manager asked Tom to tell him about his skills and experience, Tom **laid it on with a trowel.** He told the manager how great he was and boasted about his resume. He even said that while the job was beneath him he'd take it because he was easily the best person for the job.

Conversation example:

A: Poor Margaret! She's sick in bed and hasn't left the house for three days.

B: She's not sick at all. She has a cold but she's **laying it on with a trowel** for her husband.

A: Why would Margaret do a thing like that?

B: Because whenever her husband thinks she's sick he does all the housework. So, she's decided to stay in bed and let him get on with it.

 # 53 Everyday Phrase:

Laughing stock.

Meaning:

The object of derision, mockery or ridicule.

Shakespeare source:

The Merry Wives of Windsor, Act 3, scene 1.

Shakespeare quote:

SIR HUGH EVANS: Pray you let us not be **laughing-stocks** to other men's humours.

Story example:

The home team played so badly during their last three matches that they lost a total of sixty-three points and have become the **laughing stock** of the town.

Conversation example:

A: You've done a terrible job of cutting my hair. I should never have let you cut it.

B: I think it looks nice.

A: It looks dreadful. I can't leave the house like this. I'll be a **laughing stock**.

B: Do you want to borrow my hat?

 # 54 Everyday Phrase:

Lie low.

MEANING:

To stay out of sight. To bide one's time.

SHAKESPEARE SOURCE:

Much Ado About Nothing, Act 5, scene 1.

SHAKESPEARE QUOTE:

ANTONIO: If he could right himself with quarreling,
Some of us would **lie low.**

STORY EXAMPLE:

After the war, some of those responsible for crimes against humanity fled to South America where they planned to **lie low** and evade justice.

CONVERSATION EXAMPLE:

A: I just dropped mum's favourite vase.

B: You'd better clean it up immediately.

A: Yes dad.

B: And when your mother gets home, I suggest you **lie low** for a few hours.

 # 55 Everyday Phrase:

Love is blind.[11]

MEANING:

Someone in love often cannot see the imperfections and short-comings of the person they love.

11 A popular phrase today and one that Shakespeare used in several of his plays.

Shakespeare source:

Two Gentlemen of Verona, Act 2, scene 1.

Shakespeare quote:

VALENTINE: I have loved her ever since I saw her; and still I see her beautiful.

SPEED: If you love her, you cannot see her.

VALENTINE: Why?

SPEED: Because **Love is blind.**

Story example:

Mr. Hardcastle knew it was pointless trying to stop his daughter Daphne from marrying her beau. He knew **love was blind** and that she wouldn't listen to reason.

Conversation example:

A: Why is George marrying Connie Roberts?

B: Because **love is blind**.

A: **Love must be blind** because she's the most wretched woman I've ever met.

B: I agree, but unfortunately George doesn't.

 # 56 Everyday Phrase:

Melt into thin air. *(British)*

Disappear into thin air. *(American)*

Meaning:

To disappear.

Shakespeare source:

The Tempest, Act 4, scene 1.

Shakespeare quote:

PROSPERO: Our revels now are ended. These our actors,
As I foretold you, were all spirits and
Are **melted into air, into thin air.**

Story example:

The police surrounded the museum and cut off the escape routes. Inspector Hoon, the Chief of Police, thought his men had the thieves cornered but when they entered the building, the robbers and the famous Bertram diamond had **melted into thin air.**

CONVERSATION EXAMPLE:

A: Where's Robert? There's so much work to be done and he said he would help.

B: He was here a minute ago. Shall I go and look for him?

A: Don't bother. You won't find him. He always **melts into thin air** when there's hard work to be done.

 # 57 Everyday Phrase:

Method in his madness. *(British)*
Method to his madness. *(American)*

MEANING:

Expresses the idea that good results can justify unorthodox working methods.

SHAKESPEARE SOURCE:

Hamlet, Act 2, scene 2.

STORY EXAMPLE:

Although many people think the professor's working methods are strange and unusual, there is clearly **method in his madness.** His team of experts have achieved great results and made many successful scientific discoveries.

CONVERSATION EXAMPLE:

A: I think my Grandpa eats the strangest breakfast in the world.

B: What do you mean?

A: Well, every morning he eats one egg, a spoonful of hot sauce, some coconut juice and a dollop of mashed potato.

B: That sounds disgusting!

A: It is! But there must be **method in his madness** because he's a hundred and four years old and he's still as strong as an ox.

B: Tell me the recipe.

#58 Everyday Phrase:

More fool you. *(British)*

MEANING:

An expression of disapproval at a person's foolishness.

SHAKESPEARE SOURCE:

Taming of the Shrew, Act 5, scene 2.

SHAKESPEARE QUOTE:

LUCENTIO: The wisdom of your duty, fair Bianca,
Hath cost me an hundred crowns since suppertime.
BIANCA: The **more fool you** for laying on my duty.

STORY EXAMPLE:

Some teachers adopt a **'more fool you'** attitude towards students who fail to turn in homework or attend class, knowing that the student will ultimately suffer as a result of their own behavior.

CONVERSATION EXAMPLE:

A: I heard that Brad broke up with Cindy yesterday.
B: Well **more fool him** for making such a stupid decision!
A: You right. Cindy's great and any guy would be lucky to have a girlfriend like her.
B: That's so true. Have you got her phone number?

 # 59 Everyday Phrase:

Much ado about nothing.

MEANING:

A lot of fuss over nothing important.

SHAKESPEARE SOURCE:

Much Ado About Nothing—play title.

STORY EXAMPLE:

Margaret thought the latest James Bond movie was fantastic but George felt it was **much ado about nothing** and simply not worthy of all the attention and award nominations it received.

CONVERSATION EXAMPLE:

A: How was your final exam? You must have been very nervous.

B: Not really. In fact, the whole thing was **much ado about nothing.**

A: That's not what you said last week.

B: It was much easier than I had first imagined. I guess all my hard work paid off.

 # 60 Everyday Phrase:

Neither a borrower nor a lender be.

MEANING:

Don't borrow or lend if you want a good life.

SHAKESPEARE SOURCE:

Hamlet, Act 1, scene 3.

SHAKESPEARE QUOTE:

POLONIUS: **Neither a borrower nor a lender be**,
For loan oft loses both itself and friend,
And borrowing dulls the edge of husbandry.

STORY EXAMPLE:

In the current economic climate many consumers are spending less, saving more and putting faith in the old saying, **neither a lender nor a borrower be.**

CONVERSATION EXAMPLE:

A: My brother Paul still hasn't paid back the five hundred dollars I lent him last year!

B: Well, if you want some friendly advice, **neither a borrower nor a lender be!**

A: Yes, and if you have a brother who wants money, tell him to go to the bank.

Quick Quiz 6

Look at the five phrases below and the accompanying definitions. Circle TRUE or FALSE at the end of each phrase. Answers to the *Quick Quizzes* can be found at the back of the book.

1. A person who **lies low** is very short. TRUE / FALSE

2. **A laughing stock** is the object of mockery. TRUE / FALSE

3. **Love is blind** means to have multiple partners. TRUE / FALSE

4. A fuss over something unimportant is **much ado about nothing**. TRUE / FALSE

5. When a magician performs an excellent trick he **more fools you.** TRUE / FALSE

6. **The lady doth protest too much, methinks** is a common greeting among Catholic priests. TRUE / FALSE

7. **Melt into thin air** means to disappear. TRUE / FALSE

8. **Neither a borrower nor a lender be** may refer to money or possessions. TRUE / FALSE

9. Someone who is forgetful has **method in their madness** TRUE / FALSE

10. Heavily applied makeup may have been **laid on with a trowel**. TRUE / FALSE

 # 61 Everyday Phrase:

Neither here nor there

Meaning:

Of no importance or significance.

Shakespeare source:

Othello, Act 4, scene 3.

Shakespeare quote:

DESDEMONA: So, get thee gone, good night. Mine eyes do itch, Doth that bode weeping?

EMILIA: **'Tis neither here nor there.**

Story example:

Seamus was sick and tired of being sick. Life was **neither here nor there** without good health.

Conversation example:

A: What was the movie like?

B: It was **neither here nor there**.

A: How disappointing.

 # 62 Everyday Phrase:

(Neither) rhyme nor reason.

Meaning:

Without sense or meaning.

Shakespeare source:

The Comedy Of Errors, Act 2, scene 2.

Shakespeare quote:

DROMIO OF SYRACUSE: Was there ever any man thus beaten out of season, When in the "why" and the "wherefore" is neither **rhyme nor reason?**

Story example:

There was **neither rhyme nor reason** to Alice's decision to move to Scotland and study the mating habits of the Barnacle

Goose. Why Scotland? Why birds? Some of her relatives were convinced she had gone quite mad.

Conversation example:

A: Why are we having another meeting this Thursday?

B: Because the boss wants to have another meeting Thursday.

A: But there's **no rhyme nor reason** for it.

B: What the boss says, goes!

 # 63 Everyday Phrase:

Night owl.

Meaning:

A person who is habitually active late at night.

Shakespeare source:

The Rape of Lucrece, L360

Shakespeare quote:

This said, his guilty hand pluck'd up the latch,
And with his knee the door he opens wide.
The dove sleeps fast that this **night-owl** will catch:
Thus treason works ere traitors be espied.

Story example:

Feeding her baby during the night was never a problem for a **night owl** like Leila. The early mornings, however, were another story.

Conversation example:

A: What do you love most about living in New York City?

B: Well, I'm such a **night owl** that the Big Apple is the perfect place for me.

A: They say it is the city that never sleeps.

B: There's nothing I love more than sitting in a café at 3 a.m., sipping hot chocolate and watching the world go by.

 # 64 Everyday Phrase:

Not sleep/slept a wink.

Meaning:

To have no sleep.

Shakespeare source:

Cymberline, Act 3, scene 4.

Shakespeare quote:

PISANIO: O gracious lady,

Since I received command to do this business
I have not slept one wink.

Story example:

Bonny was so nervous that she **didn't sleep a wink** the night before her interview. Luckily, the interview went well and she got the job.

Conversation example:

A: What's wrong? You look so tired.

B: I **haven't slept a wink** this week.

A: How come?

B: The woman next door has just given birth to triplets.

 # 65 Everyday Phrase:

One fell swoop.[12]

Meaning:

To do something or several things suddenly and all at once.

Shakespeare source:

Macbeth, Act 4, scene 3.

Shakespeare quote:

MACDUFF: Did you say all? O hell-kite! All?

What, all my pretty chickens and their dam
At one fell swoop?

---

12 This phrase is commonly misquoted as "*one foul swoop*" or "*one false swoop*" or even "*one fall swoop*." Macduff likens his murdered family to little chicks that have been killed by a bird of prey. The word "fell" has different meanings today but in this 16th century context the word meant "dreadful, terrible."

Story example:

There were three biscuits left on the plate; one for Tommy; one for his sister; one for his mother. Suddenly, Tommy's older brother, Bill, appeared and in **one fell swoop** grabbed all three biscuits and devoured them greedily.

Conversation example:

A: Why aren't you doing your homework?

B: Because I'm watching television.

A: But you have four essays to finish by Tuesday morning.

B: I plan to do them in **one fell swoop** on Sunday afternoon.

 # 66 Everyday Phrase:

Own flesh and blood.

Meaning:

Family/Used to express the importance of family.

Shakespeare source:

Merchant of Venice, Act 3, scene 1.

Shakespeare quote:

SHYLOCK: She is damned for it.

SOLANIO: That's certain—if the devil may be her judge.

SHYLOCK: My **own flesh and blood** to rebel!

Story example:

After the funeral, Mrs. Jonson's greedy relatives gathered to hear a lawyer read her will. They were shocked to learn that Mrs. Jonson hadn't left anything to her **own flesh blood.** They were even more shocked to learn that she had left her entire fortune to Duncan, her beloved cat.

Conversation example:

A: I hear there's a job opening in the finance department. I know the manager. I think you should apply for it.

B: I'll go and see him right now. Thanks, Uncle.

A: Don't mention it. You're my **own flesh and blood.** I'll do anything to help you.

67 Everyday Phrase:

Pitched battle.

MEANING:

A fierce battle between opposing forces.

SHAKESPEARE SOURCE:

Taming of the Shrew, Act 1, scene 2.

SHAKESPEARE QUOTE:

PETRUCHIO: Have I not in a **pitched battle** heard
Loud 'larums, neighing steeds, and trumpets' clang?
And do you tell me of a woman's tongue,
That gives not half so great a blow to hear
As will a chestnut in a farmer's fire?
Tush, tush! fear boys with bugs.

STORY EXAMPLE:

What started as a peaceful protest soon turned violent. Police arrested dozens of people and by nightfall the demonstration had become a **pitched battle** between police and protestors.

CONVERSATION EXAMPLE:

A: You look tired.

B: That's because my neighbors had a terrible argument last night. It sounded like a **pitched battle** right above my head.

A: That's love!

B: Remind me never to get married.

68 Everyday Phrase:

Play fast and loose.

MEANING:

To do something in a reckless way/to be willfully neglectful.

SHAKESPEARE SOURCE:

King John, Act 3, scene 1.

SHAKESPEARE QUOTE:

KING PHILIP: And shall these hands, so lately purged of blood,
So newly join'd in love, so strong in both,

Unyoke this seizure and this kind regreet?
Play fast and loose with faith?

Story example:

Most tabloid newspapers **play fast and loose** with the facts. Many people believe that such newspapers care more about selling copies than reporting the news accurately.

Conversation example:

A: I thought Justin was married.

B: He is.

A: But he told me has a girlfriend.

B: Unfortunately, Justin **plays fast and loose** with his marriage and faith.

A: I feel sorry for his poor wife.

 # 69 Everyday Phrase:

Pomp and circumstance.

Meaning:

Grandiose ceremonies and formal celebrations.

Shakespeare source:

Othello, Act 3, scene 3.

Shakespeare quote:

OTHELLO: Farewell the neighing steed and the shrill trump,
The spirit-stirring drum, th' ear-piercing fife,
The royal banner, and all quality,
Pride, **pomp, and circumstance** of glorious war!

Story example:

The homecoming celebrations were accompanied by a great deal of **pomp and circumstance.** Before the Lord Mayor's presentation ceremony, a marching band led the team on a victory parade through the streets of London.

Conversation example:

A: Did you watch the royal wedding?

B: Yes and didn't they look lovely?

A: Everything looked lovely.

B: It must have cost a fortune.

A: **Pomp and circumstance** is never cheap.

70 Everyday Phrase:

Pound of flesh.

MEANING:

A debt that a lender harshly demands knowing that it will cause suffering to the payer.

SHAKESPEARE SOURCE:

Merchant of Venice, Act 4, scene 1.

SHAKESPEARE QUOTE:

SHYLOCK: The **pound of flesh** which I demand of him
Is dearly bought. 'Tis mine and I will have it.
If you deny me, fie upon your law—

STORY EXAMPLE:

Jason's landlord got his **pound of flesh** the day Jason moved out by keeping Jason's entire deposit. He refused to give the money back because Jason had damaged the furniture, broken a door and left the apartment in a complete mess.

CONVERSATION EXAMPLE:

A: Principal Jones?

B: How can I help you Dr. Smith?

A: I know you think Sam Edwards has great potential but today is the third time I've caught him misbehaving in my science class and I want my **pound of flesh**.

B: Well, I suggest you give him extra homework and detention for the next three weeks.

Quick Quiz 7

Decide which idiom or phrase best fits the blank spaces in the sentences below.

1. John was so nervous that he had ____________________ for the whole week before the operation.
2. Marjorie had always been a ____________________ so getting up in the morning was always a problem.
3. The king enjoyed the ____________________ of a big public ceremony.
4. Their divorce was like a ____________________ between two warring armies.
5. He treated his adopted family like his ______________.
6. Betty was going to take her cheating rat of an ex-husband and get her ____________________.
7. An accident was inevitable the way the company played ____________________with safety.
8. During the battle the village lost an entire generation in ____________________.
9. It's no surprise the restaurant closed down. The food was ____________________.
10. What Ben did was totally out of character and there seemed to be ____________________ for his behavior.

 # 71 Everyday Phrase:

The Queen's English (or the King's English when a male monarch sits on the English throne).

MEANING:

To speak with clarity, good diction and perfect grammar.

SHAKESPEARE SOURCE:

The Merry Wives of Windsor, Act 1, scene 4.

SHAKESPEARE QUOTE:

MISTRESS QUICKLY: What, John Rugby! I pray thee, go to the casement, and see if you can see my master, Master Doctor Caius, coming. If he do, i' faith, and find any body in the house, here will be an old abusing of God's patience and the **king's English.**

STORY EXAMPLE:

Many teenagers are perfectly capable of speaking **the Queen's English** but choose to break grammar rules and use slang in order to fit in with their peers.

CONVERSATION EXAMPLE:

A: How's it hanging bro?

B: You mean, Hi dad, how are you?

A: Wasssup? You need a translator?

B: Not if you speak the **Queen's English.**

 # 72 Everyday Phrase:

Refuse to budge an inch.

MEANING:

Totally refuse to cooperate.

SHAKESPEARE SOURCE:

Taming of the Shrew, Induction, scene 1.

SHAKESPEARE QUOTE:

HOSTESS: You will not pay for the glasses you have burst?

SLY: No, not a denier. Go by, Saint Jeronimy! go to thy cold bed, and warm thee.

HOSTESS: I know my remedy; I must go fetch the thirdborough.

[Exit]

SLY: Third, or fourth, or fifth borough, I'll answer him by law. **I'll not budge an inch**, boy; let him come and kindly.

Story example:

Mr. and Mrs. Jones had a terrible time when they stayed at the Villa Hotel last summer. Their room was dirty, the staff rude and the shower in the bathroom didn't work. When Mr. Jones demanded a refund the manager **refused to budge an inch**. He told Mr. Jones that if he didn't like the hotel he should go and find somewhere else to stay.

Conversation example:

A: Hi John, are you going to the party tomorrow night?

B: If I finish my homework, I will go.

A: Forget homework!

B: I can't. My mother said that if I don't finish it I'm not going and she **refuses to budge an inch**.

 # 73 Everyday Phrase:

Salad days.

Meaning:

Referring to youthful inexperience.

Shakespeare source:

Antony and Cleopatra, Act 1, scene 5.

Shakespeare quote:

CLEOPATRA: **My salad days,**
When I was green in judgment: cold in blood.

Story example:

Whenever a junior member of staff did something stupid, Mr. Peebles, the boss, tried to be patient. He would remember the mistakes of his own **salad days**, like the time he sent a package for London, England to London, Ontario. Or the time he send a package for Birmingham, England to Birmingham, Alabama.

CONVERSATION EXAMPLE:

A: It's the middle of winter and my teenage son wants to go to school in a t-shirt and shorts.

B: My teenage daughter goes to bed too late every night and wonders why she can't get up in the morning.

A: I guess that's what **salad days** are for; making mistakes and learning from them.

 # 74 Everyday Phrase:

Sea change.

MEANING:

A transformation or significant change in opinion, belief thought, policy, direction etc.

SHAKESPEARE SOURCE:

The Tempest, Act 1, scene 2.

SHAKESPEARE QUOTE:

ARIEL: *(sings)* Full fathom five thy father lies.
Of his bones are coral made.
Those are pearls that were his eyes.
Nothing of him that doth fade,
But doth suffer a **sea-change**
Into something rich and strange.
Sea-nymphs hourly ring his knell.

STORY EXAMPLE:

After Mr. Rosen's heart attack he quit smoking, gave up junk food and started going to the local gym. It was a real **sea change** for Mr. Rosen who never used to care about his health.

CONVERSATION EXAMPLE:

A: Why are you moving to the suburbs? I thought you loved living downtown.

B: It's a bit of a **sea change** for me but after all these years in the city I'm ready for some peace and quiet.

A: Then I guess moving to the suburbs is the right decision for you.

 # 75 Everyday Phrase:

Seen better days.

Meaning:

Past one's prime. Fallen into decline. In worse condition than in past times.

Shakespeare source:

Timon of Athens, Act 4, scene 2.

Shakespeare quote:

FLAVIUS: Let's yet be fellows; let's shake our heads, and say,
As 'twere a knell unto our master's fortunes,
'We have **seen better days.'**

Story example:

All the employees were worried about the boss, Mr. Stein. He never took a break, slept at his desk most days and hadn't taken a vacation in years. He certainly looked like he had **seen better days.**

Conversation example:

A: You're not wearing that suit to the party tonight, are you?

B: Why? What's wrong with it?

A: To tell you the truth, it looks like it's **seen better days**. When did you buy it?

B: 1974.

 # 76 Everyday Phrase:

Send (someone) packing.

Meaning:

To send someone away, to dismiss someone.

Shakespeare source:

Henry IV, Part I, Act 2, scene 4.

Shakespeare quote:

FALSTAFF: What doth Gravity out of his bed at midnight? Shall I give him his answer?

PRINCE HENRY: Prithee do, Jack.

FALSTAFF: Faith, and I'll **send him packing.**

STORY EXAMPLE:

James had received several attractive offers to play for other clubs but had **sent them all packing**. He was loyal to his club, had always worn The Reds shirt with pride and always would.

CONVERSATION EXAMPLE:

A: How is your new neighbor?

B: The landlord's **sent her packing** already.

A: Really? Why?

B: Because she decided to have a party every day last week until 3 a.m.

 # 77 Everyday Phrase:

Set one's teeth on edge.

MEANING:

To cause great irritation or feeling of unpleasantness.

SHAKESPEARE SOURCE:

Henry IV, Part I, Act 3, scene 1.

SHAKESPEARE QUOTE:

HOTSPUR: And that would **set my teeth nothing an edge**,
Nothing so much as mincing poetry.
'Tis like the forced gait of a shuffling nag.

STORY EXAMPLE:

As the 134 bus to Muswell Hill rounded the corner, the brakes made a terrible screeching noise that **set everybody's teeth on edge.**

CONVERSATION EXAMPLE:

A: Could you stop doing that please?

B: Stop doing what?

A: Dragging the desk across the floor. The noise really **sets my teeth on edge.**

B: I'm sorry. I didn't realize it bothered you so much.

 # 78 Everyday Phrase:

The short and long of it.[13]

MEANING:

In summary/the gist of something.

SHAKESPEARE SOURCE:

The Merry Wives of Windsor, Act 2, scene 2.

SHAKESPEARE QUOTE:

MISTRESS QUICKLY: Marry, this is **the short and the long of it;** you have brought her into such a canaries as 'tis wonderful.

STORY EXAMPLE:

Mary didn't have time to read the entire novel before her class so she read the summary and hoped to get **the short and long of it.**

CONVERSATION EXAMPLE:

A: Hi Jeff! How was the honeymoon?

B: Fantastic, thanks.

A: I want to hear all about it. Where did you stay? What did you do? Was the weather good?

B: It was wonderful from start to finish. That's **the short and long of it.**

 # 79 Everyday Phrase:

Short shrift.

MEANING:

To give little or no consideration to a person or idea.

SHAKESPEARE SOURCE:

Richard III, Act 3, scene 4.

SHAKESPEARE QUOTE:

RATCLIFFE: Come, come, dispatch. The duke would be at dinner. Make a **short shrift.** He longs to see your head.

---

13 Commonly changed to "*The long and short of it.*"

STORY EXAMPLE:

In the beginning, many of her ideas were given **short shrift** simply because she was a woman. Later, she would rise to become the CEO, proving herself and her ideas worthy of respect and admiration.

CONVERSATION EXAMPLE:

A: What did Mr. Jonson say about your raise?

B: He gave me and my proposal **short shrift.**

A: I'm sorry to hear that.

B: Not as sorry as I was.

 # 80 Everyday Phrase:

Something is rotten in the state of Denmark.

MEANING:

To suggest or refer to political corruption or wrongdoing.

SHAKESPEARE SOURCE:

Hamlet, Act 1, scene 4.

SHAKESPEARE QUOTE:

MARCELLUS: *(Seeing the ghost of Hamlet's father)* Something is **rotten in the state of Denmark.**

STORY EXAMPLE:

Several opposition leaders have mysteriously disappeared in recent months and many suspect government involvement. Furthermore, the President's victory was announced before the ballots were counted. People know there's **something rotten in the state of Denmark** but are too frightened to speak out.

CONVERSATION EXAMPLE:

A: Have you heard the news? Victoria Swanson has been arrested.

B: Arrested? What for?

A: Apparently, she and several other managers have been stealing money from the company for years.

B: **Something rotten in the state of Denmark!** I knew it!

Quick Quiz 8

What idioms or phrases best match the descriptions below.

1. To order someone away.
2. To be extremely stubborn and not agree to change one's opinion.
3. Something that is worn and tatty.
4. A model of good speech.
5. Dismissiveness.
6. All is not well in society!
7. An about-face.
8. In summary.
9. Cause an annoyance.
10. A time of youthful inexperience.

 # 81 Everyday Phrase:

A sorry sight.

MEANING:
A sight/person/thing that is pitiful or unpleasant to behold.

SHAKESPEARE SOURCE:
Macbeth, Act 2, scene 2.

SHAKESPEARE QUOTE:
MACBETH: *(Looking at his bloody hands)* **This is a sorry sight**.

STORY EXAMPLE:
After the match the players left the pitch. Defeated, they looked utterly miserable and broken. It was the **sorriest of sights** for the home fans but not for the visitors who added another victory to their impressive record.

CONVERSATION EXAMPLE:
A: Michael, you forgot to feed the dog again!
B: I did?
A: Yes you did. And you left him in the yard all day in the pouring rain.
B: Oh.
A: He looked such **a sorry sight** when I got home that I could have cried.
B: Well, I guess I'm the one who's in the dog house tonight.

 # 82 Everyday Phrase:

A spotless reputation.

MEANING:
A reputation that is very good.

SHAKESPEARE SOURCE:
Richard II, Act 1, scene 1.

SHAKESPEARE QUOTE:
THOMAS MOWBRAY: The purest treasure mortal times afford
Is **spotless reputation:** that away,
Men are but gilded loam or painted clay.

Story example:

Unlike most politicians, Senator Hughes has a **spotless reputation**. As such, he is an ideal candidate for the presidency.

Conversation example:

B: I really can't decide who should get the job.

A: I agree. The top two candidates both have a lot of skills and so much experience.

B: Yes and they both have **spotless reputations** in the industry.

 # 83 Everyday Phrase:

Stony hearted. *(British)*
Stone hearted. *(American)*

Meaning:

Uncaring, cruel, unkind.

Shakespeare source:

Henry IV, Part I, Act 2, scene 2.

Shakespeare quote:

FALSTAFF: Eight yards of uneven ground is threescore and ten miles afoot with me, and the **stony-hearted** villains know it well enough. A plague upon it when thieves cannot be true one to another!

Story example:

Since losing his job, Maxwell hasn't been able to pay his bills on time. He phoned the utility company to explain his situation but all he got was a stony-hearted response.

Conversation example:

B: My husband never buys me flowers, always forgets our anniversary and rarely pays me a compliment.

A: Does he have a memory problem?

B: No, he's just **stony hearted.**

A: You poor thing.

 # 84 Everyday Phrase:

Strange bedfellows.

Meaning:

An unusual alliance or partnership, often in pursuit of a shared goal.

Shakespeare source:

The Tempest, Act 2, scene 2.

Shakespeare quote:

TRINCULO: Alas, the storm is come again! My best way is to creep under his gaberdine. There is no other shelter hereabouts. Misery acquaints a man with **strange bedfellows.** I will here shroud till the dregs of the storm be past.

Story example:

Rock guitarist Harry 'Hellraiser' Harrison and Father Norman Maybury from Saint Giles' Church are **strange bedfellows** indeed! The two men have joined forces to fight government plans for a new housing development in the small village of Lipsbury Pinfold where the two men live.

Conversation example:

A: George and Janet really do make **strange bedfellows**, don't they?

B: Yes they do. He's a ninety-three-year-old retired soldier and she's a beautiful, young peace protestor from Columbia.

B: They're an odd couple but they work together in the community because they both care so much about helping homeless people.

A: I see. Now I understand.

 # 85 Everyday Phrase:

That way madness lies.

Meaning:

A proposed or suggested course of action will end in disaster or insanity.

Shakespeare source:

King Lear, Act 3, scene 4.

Shakespeare quote:

LEAR: No, I will weep no more. In such a night

To shut me out! Pour on, I will endure.

In such a night as this! O Regan, Goneril,
Your old kind father, whose frank heart gave all—
Oh, **that way madness lies.** Let me shun that.
No more of that.

Story example:

Choosing the safer route, Mr. Slocum sailed his boat eastward. He knew that a north-easterly route would have been quicker but **that way madness lies**. Only the most foolhardy of sailors sail directly into the path of a storm.

Conversation example:

A: Isn't Penny such a lovely girl?
B: Yes she is but **that way madness lies.**
A: What do you mean?
B: She's twenty years younger than you, will break your heart and leave you penniless.

 # 86 Everyday Phrase:

Thereby hangs a tale.

Meaning:

There's a more detailed and longer story behind the subject currently being discussed.

Shakespeare source:

As You Like It, Act 2, scene 7.

Shakespeare quote:

JAQUES: 'Thus we may see,' quoth he, 'how the world wags:
'Tis but an hour ago since it was nine,
And after one hour more 'twill be eleven;
And so, from hour to hour, we ripe and ripe,
And then, from hour to hour, we rot and rot;
And **thereby hangs a tale.'**

Story example:

Mr. Roberts had been a prisoner at Holloway prison for several years and **thereby hangs a very murky tale** but today he is just visiting, a reformed character and a free man, dedicated to helping others.

Conversation example:

A: I love your hat. Is it new?

B: No, no, I've had it for years. I just don't wear it often.

B: Really? Why not?

A: It reminds me of Paris, the summer of '96 . . . and **thereby hangs a tale**.

 # 87 Everyday Phrase:

Throw cold water on it.

Meaning:

To discourage or to thwart.

Shakespeare source:

The Merry Wives of Windsor, Act 2, scene 3.

Shakespeare quote:

HOST: Let him die: sheathe thy impatience, **throw cold water on** thy choler: go about the fields with me through Frogmore.

Story example:

Mr. Hampton was determined to **throw cold water on** his daughter's plans to marry. She was too young and he would find a way to stop her.

Conversation example:

A: What happened at the office party?

B: We didn't have an office party this year.

A: But I thought you were planning it.

B: I was but the boss said it was too expensive and **threw cold water on it.**

 # 88 Everyday Phrase:

To be or not to be.[14]

14 Shakespeare's most famous line and indeed probably all of literature's most famous line.

Meaning:

To live or die?

Shakespeare source:

Hamlet, Act 3, scene 1.

Shakespeare quote:

HAMLET: **To be, or not to be?** That is the question—
Whether 'tis nobler in the mind to suffer
The slings and arrows of outrageous fortune,
Or to take arms against a sea of troubles,
And, by opposing, end them?

Story example:

Bob was sick, broken-hearted and poor. He tried to be positive but today was one of those **to be or not to be** days in life when he wondered if it was all worth it.

Conversation example:

A: Jackie just broke up with me. I feel miserable.

B: **To be or not to be.**

A: Life's so difficult sometimes.

B: Be positive. You never know what tomorrow will bring.

 # 89 Everyday Phrase:

Too much of a good thing.

Meaning:

Indulgence can be bad for you.

Shakespeare source:

As You Like It, Act 4, scene 1.

Shakespeare quote:

ROSALIND: Why then, can one desire **too much of a good thing?** Come, sister, you shall be the priest and marry us.—Give me your hand, Orlando. What do you say, sister?

Story example:

The seventy-seven-year-old oil magnate died of a heart attack during a moment of passion with his thirty-year-old girlfriend.

He may have believed that a younger woman would keep him youthful but it proved **too much of a good thing** in the end.

Conversation example:

A: I'm drinking because my doctor told me that red wine is good for your health.

B: Yes but you should be careful.

A: What on earth do you mean?

B: A glass of wine a day is good for you but a bottle a day is **too much of a good thing.**

 # 90 Everyday Phrase:

Tongue-tied.

Meaning:

Speechless or confused speech usually as the result of shyness, embarrassment or nervousness.

Shakespeare source:

A Midsummer Night's Dream, Act 5, scene 1.

Shakespeare quote:

THESEUS: Love, therefore, and **tongue-tied** simplicity
In least speak most, to my capacity.

Story example:

Ralph dreaded giving presentations at work. Even when reading from notes he would become horribly **tongue-tied**, stammering and stuttering his way through the meeting.

Conversation example:

A: Teacher, I understand grammar but when I speak I always get **tongue-tied.**

B: Don't worry about it. Even the teacher gets **tongue-tied** sometimes.

B: The teacher gets **tongue-tied**?

A: The next time the attractive new Level 3 teacher comes and talks to me, you'll see what I mean.

Quick Quiz 9

Circle the incorrect word in each phrase and write the correct phrase in the space provided.

1. Sorry sound. ______________________.
2. Throw hot water on it. ______________________.
3. Strange roomfellows. ______________________.
4. Thereby hands a tale. ______________________.
5. That way madmen lie. ______________________.
6. A spotty reputation. ______________________.
7. 2B or not 2B. ______________________.
8. Story hearted. ______________________.
9. Tong-tied. ______________________.
10. Too much of a bad thing. ______________________.

91 Everyday Phrase:

To the manner born.[15]

MEANING:

A natural aptitude for something due to background, practice, exposure etc.

SHAKESPEARE SOURCE:

Hamlet, Act 1, scene 4.

SHAKESPEARE QUOTE:

HAMLET: But to my mind, though I am native here
And **to the manner born**, it is a custom
More honored in the breach than the observance.

STORY EXAMPLE:

Boxing was in Mickey's blood. His father and grandfather had both boxed professionally and Mickey had spent so much time watching and studying the art of boxing that by the time he stepped into the ring himself it was clear for all to see that he was **to the manner born.**

CONVERSATION EXAMPLE:

A: Did you hear the news? Patrick has been offered a movie contract.

B: That's wonderful but I'm not surprised.

A: Both his parents were actors, weren't they?

B: Yes and he practically grew up on movie sets. He's **to the manner born**.

---

15 This phrase is frequently misunderstood by native speakers to mean "*from a wealthy or privileged background.*" Such misinterpretation occurs because the word "manner" has the same pronunciation as "manor" in English. The distinction between these two different words and their separate meanings, clear to us on the written page, is lost in spoken English and many native speakers assume the phrase is "*to the **manor** born.*" The association of a large country house or "*manor*" with wealth and prestige is an obvious one. Consequently, misinterpretation arises.

 # 92 Everyday Phrase:

To thine own self be true.

Meaning:

Be yourself.

Shakespeare source:

Hamlet, Act 1, scene 3.

Shakespeare quote:

POLONIUS: Neither a borrower nor a lender be;
For loan oft loses both itself and friend,
And borrowing dulls the edge of husbandry.
This above all: **to thine own self be true.**

Story example:

His father's advice before he left for college was **to thine own self be true.**
It took a long time and many mistakes for Joey to understand this but at last he knew that if he stood by the values he held dear, people would respect him, even if they didn't always agree with him.

Conversation example:

A: Can you give me some advice before my interview.

B: Sure. **To thine own self be true.**

A: You mean don't inflate my resume?

B: Yes and be yourself.

 # 93 Everyday Phrase:

A tower of strength.

Meaning:

A person who gives support and comfort in hard times.

Shakespeare source:

Richard III, Act, 5, scene 3.

Shakespeare quote:

RICHARD: Up with my tent!—Here will I lie tonight. But where tomorrow? Well, all's one for that. Who hath descried the number of the traitors?

NORFOLK: Six or seven thousand is their utmost power.

RICHARD: Why, our battalia trebles that account.
Besides, the king's name is **a tower of strength**
Which they upon the adverse party want.

STORY EXAMPLE:

After Richard's divorce his friend Karen was **a tower of strength**. She took the kids to school in the mornings so he could find a new apartment and was always there when he needed someone to talk to.

CONVERSATION EXAMPLE:

A: Thanks for helping me out when I lost my job last year.

B: You're welcome.

A: You were a **tower of strength.**

B: That's what friends are for.

 # 94 Everyday Phrase:

Truth will out.

MEANING:

The truth will always emerge even if it is hidden for many years.

SHAKESPEARE SOURCE:

Merchant of Venice, Act 2, scene 1.

SHAKESPEARE QUOTE:

LAUNCELOT: Well, old man, I will tell you news of your son. Give me your blessing. Truth will come to light. Murder cannot be hid long—a man's son may, but in the end **truth will out.**

STORY EXAMPLE:

After many years in prison for a crime he did not commit, Mr. Jackson was finally freed thanks to DNA evidence. He told reporters that he always believed that one day the **truth would out** and after a long wait it finally did.

CONVERSATION EXAMPLE:

A: The boss' son arrives thirty minutes late every morning.

B: And he leaves early every day.

A: He's so lazy he shouldn't have a job.

B: Don't worry. The company inspectors are making a secret visit next week. Then **the truth will out**.

 # 95 Everyday Phrase:

Up in arms.

Meaning:

Outraged, incensed.

Shakespeare source:

Richard III, Act 4, scene 4.

Shakespeare quote:

RICHARD: March on, march on, since we are **up in arms,**
If not to fight with foreign enemies,
Yet to beat down these rebels here at home.

Story example:

According to reports, the Lord Mayor is **up in arms** over government plans to curb his powers.

Conversation example:

A: The workers are on strike.

B: Why?

A: Because they got a pay cut while the management received a six percent raise.

B: Well, it's no surprise they are **up in arms** about the situation.

 # 96 Everyday Phrase:

Vanish into thin air.[16]
Disappear into thin air. *(American)*

Meaning:

To disappear.

16 This phrase is a variation of the phrase "***Melt*** *into thin air,*" which appears in Shakespeare's *The Tempest* (and can also be found in this book).

SHAKESPEARE SOURCE:

Othello, Act 3, scene 1.

SHAKESPEARE QUOTE:

CLOWN: Then put up your pipes in your bag, for I'll away: go; **vanish into air;** away!

STORY EXAMPLE:

Jessica's teenage son loves to eat. Dinner time is his favorite part of the day but he **vanishes into thin air** when it's time to clear the table and do the dishes.

CONVERSATION EXAMPLE:

A: Whose turn is it to buy the drinks?

B: It's Jerry's turn. He was here a minute ago. Where did he go?

A: He's **vanished into thin air** again.

 # 97 Everyday Phrase:

Wear one's heart upon one's sleeve.

MEANING:

To openly display one's emotions and feelings.

SHAKESPEARE SOURCE:

Othello. Act 1, scene 1.

SHAKESPEARE QUOTE:

IAGO: For when my outward action doth demonstrate
The native act and figure of my heart
In compliment extern, 'tis not long after
But I will **wear my heart upon my sleeve**
For daws to peck at. I am not what I am.

STORY EXAMPLE:

Bill's Auntie Cassandra is a famous opera singer who lives in Italy. Everyone in the family thinks Cassandra is very dramatic. **She certainly wears her heart on her sleeve**. When she's angry, she screams and shouts. When she's sad, she's in floods of tears. She never hides her feelings and Bill thinks that makes her a very honest person.

Conversation example:

A: I see Jack is in love again.

B: How do you know Jack's in love?

A: Because he always **wears his heart on his sleeve**. Look at him!

B: Yes, now you mention it he does seem very happy and he's been dancing around the kitchen all morning.

 # 98 Everyday Phrase:

What a piece of work is man!

Meaning:

Man is a wonder!

(Used ironically, this phrase has also come to mean the direct opposite: How terrible Man is!)

Shakespeare source:

Hamlet, Act 2, scene 2.

Shakespeare quote:

HAMLET: **What a piece of work is a man!**

How noble in reason, how infinite in faculty!
In form and moving how express and admirable!
In action how like an angel, in apprehension how like a god!
The beauty of the world.
The paragon of animals.
And yet, to me, what is this quintessence of dust?

Story example:

What a piece of work is man, Aunt Mabel would think whenever she visited The National Gallery and marveled at the extraordinary artwork on display.

Conversation example:

A: We must never forget The Genocide.

B: We never will.

A: But we can forgive.

B: **What a piece of work is man**!

 # 99 Everyday Phrase:

What's done is done.

MEANING:
We cannot change the past (and therefore should accept it).

SHAKESPEARE SOURCE:
Macbeth, Act 3, scene 2.

SHAKESPEARE QUOTE:
LADY MACBETH: How now, my lord! Why do you keep alone,
Of sorriest fancies your companions making,
Using those thoughts which should indeed have died
With them they think on? Things without all remedy
Should be without regard. **What's done is done.**

STORY EXAMPLE:
Melissa wishes with all her heart that she had never had the party at her parents' house when they were out of town. **What's done is done** and she will work hard to pay for the damage and even harder to rebuild the trust between them.

CONVERSATION EXAMPLE:
A: Are you okay? I heard you failed the exam.
B: Yes but it's my own fault, I didn't study and skipped class a lot.
A: What are you going to do?
B: I don't know but **what's done is done**. If I change my attitude maybe I can pass next time.

 # 100 Everyday Phrase:

Wild goose chase.

MEANING:
A fruitless or unsatisfactory pursuit or search.

SHAKESPEARE SOURCE:
Romeo and Juliet, Act 2, scene 4.

Shakespeare quote:

MERCUTIO: Nay, if our wits run the **wild-goose chase**, I am done, for thou hast more of the wild-goose in one of thy wits than, I am sure, I have in my whole five.

Story example:

Kimberly searched just about every store in town for the ingredients to her grandmother's famous fruit cake. After many hours, she returned home empty-handed. The whole day had been one big **wild goose chase.**

Conversation example:

A: I can't believe it!

B: What?

A: Bernard just called to tell me he'd picked up my cell phone last night by mistake and taken it home.

A: Well, you should be happy.

B: Yes but I wasted an entire day on a **wild goose chase** looking for it.

 # 101 Everyday Phrase:

The world's my oyster.

Meaning:

Great opportunities and pleasures are open to you.

Shakespeare source:

The Merry Wives of Windsor, Act 2, scene 2.

Shakespeare quote:

FALSTAFF: I will not lend thee a penny.

PISTOL: Why, then **the world's mine oyster.** Which I with sword will open.

Story example:

Tommy felt wonderful after the graduation ceremony. He shook hands with his father and hugged his mother. He had finally graduated and with a first-class degree from a top university. He felt like **the world was his oyster** and that he could achieve anything.

Conversation example:

A: Gramps, what do you miss most about being young?

B: I miss so many things.

A: Like what?

B: When you're young you can do anything, go anywhere, **the world is your oyster**.

A: **Is the world my oyster**, Gramps?

B: Yes it is and I hope you enjoy every moment of it.

Quick Quiz 10

Choose the correct answers from the multiple choice list below:

1. To be up in arms suggests your mood is . . .

a) relaxed
b) nervous
c) romantic
d) angry

2. A wild goose chase is a search for . . .

a) goose
b) something you will never find
c) a rainbow
d) tranquility

3. A tower of strength is . . .

a) a strong building
b) a safe deposit box
c) a reliabe friend
d) a gym

4. If the world is my oyster I am probably not . . .

a) very old
b) young
c) hopeful
d) positive

5. If I wear my heart on my sleeve then I must . . .

a) be fashionable
b) have bad table manners
c) easily show my feelings
d) be a doctor or surgeon

6. If I vanish into thin air then I have . . .

a) disappeared
b) lost too much weight
c) eaten too much
d) bad lungs

7. To the manner born suggests a person . . .

a) is rich
b) is naturally talented
c) was born at home
d) has good manners

8. To thine own self be true advises us to . . .

a) be courageous
b) be brave
c) be strong
d) be ourselves

9. The truth will out suggests that . . .

a) lying achieves one's aims
b) people are truthful
c) truth hurts
d) justice will prevail

10. What a piece of work man is suggests man is . . .

a) insiginificat
b) noble
c) wonderful
d) strong

11. What's done is done means . . .

a) do it well
b) we cannot change the past
c) we need to do something
d) I did something yesterday

An ESL Shakespeare Love Story:
A Tale Of Betrayal, Heartache, And The English Language

What follows is some lighthearted fun: a dialogue based on some of the *101 Phrases* that you have just read. More than half of all the idioms and phrases in this book appear in this one dialogue! Can you find them all? More importantly, do you understand the conversation from beginning to end? You can use the book to check the meaning of the phrases you find in the conversation, which demonstrates the everyday use of such phrases in the context of an informal conversation between two friends.

It isn't exactly Shakespeare . . . well, okay, it is Shakespeare. Read the conversation out loud with a partner. Then read the dialogue again changing roles. When you're finished create your own dialogue based on the phrases and idioms in this book. You'll have a lot of fun doing it and it will help to strengthen your understanding of the phrases you use.

Start by making a simple conversation that uses three or four of the phrases, then add more as you grow in confidence. Good luck!

A: You look like a sorry sight. What's up?

B: I've seen better days, that's true. I didn't sleep a wink last night.

A: I didn't know you were a night owl.

B: I'm not.

A: So why haven't you slept a wink?

B: Well, thereby hangs a tale. The short and the long of it is that my girlfriend sent me packing yesterday.

A: Oh dear! The course of true love never runs smooth, does it?!

B: I thought I had a charmed life. I thought we would be together forever and a day.

A: A broken heart isn't the be all and end all. What's done is done. Besides, you're fancy-free now.

B: That's cold comfort, I'm afraid. I thought she was as pure as the driven snow. Love really is blind, I guess. Do you think I can win her back?

A: Look, I'm going to be cruel but only to be kind. It sounds like your love is as dead as a doornail.

B: You're right! She dashed our love to pieces and behaved like the devil incarnate with the next door neighbor!

A: Good riddance to her!

B: I was never a green-eyed monster, even when that hot-blooded young man moved into the apartment upstairs.

A: More fool you.

B: I asked her why she spent so much time talking to him the day he moved in, but she said she was just breaking the ice.

A: What? You didn't think her story stank to high heaven?

B: No, I didn't suspect foul-play for one minute. I believed her improbable fiction.

A: She was playing fast and loose with the facts, wasn't she?! And now you're in a right pickle.

B: I was up in arms when I found out. Her behavior beggars all description. I wanted my pound of flesh, alright. When she realized the game was up she broke down and cried.

A: I suspect she laid it on with a trowel to try and make you feel bad.

B: She was waiting with bated breath for me to take her back.

A: I hope you gave her short shrift. Come what come may, you mustn't take her back.

B: If I did, I'd be the laughing stock of the entire apartment block.

A: It's time to fight fire with fire and get a new girlfriend.

B: Perhaps I should just lie low for a few weeks.

A: No. That way madness lies.

B: Well, as good luck would have it, at the same time the new neighbor moved in upstairs, a very nice young lady moved into the apartment downstairs.

A: It's high time you introduced yourself to her.

B: Do you really think so?

A: It's a foregone conclusion. In a few weeks all this heartache will seem much ado about nothing.

B: You mean, my sadness will melt into thin air?

A: Precisely.

B: But I can't introduce myself to her because I always get tongue-tied when I meet new girls.

A: Don't throw cold water on the plan before you've even met her.

B: Perhaps I could tell her a few 'knock, knock, who's there?' jokes.

A: An excellent idea! You'll have her in stitches. You'll soon forget all about that stony hearted ex-girlfriend. But don't gild the lily with the jokes. Remember, brevity is the soul of wit. The world's your oyster.

B: Thanks. You've been a tower of strength.

A: You're welcome. There's a brave new world out there waiting for you!

Romeo And Juliet: The Ten Minute ESL Version

Bravo! And since we are on theme of Love, let's continue with an ESL version of Shakespeare's classic love story . . . for ESL students.

One of the challenges of the ESL classroom is getting students to speak with confidence and surety. The direct focus of the teacher and fellow students in a classroom setting can be a daunting experience for the reluctant speaker.

Common classroom techniques to free up speech inhibition engage students in activities with a different focus, thus reducing the level of self-consciousness students sometimes feel when speaking.

These techniques might include simple games or activities such as throwing and catching a ball while practicing spoken exercises, or perhaps reciting grammar exercises while walking around the classroom with a partner.

Role-playing too is a useful technique that connects students to spoken English in an active way, but without the prescriptive approach to pronunciation and grammar rules that many teachers employ in a traditional classroom setting.

Acting out the AB dialogues in the 101 section of this book will help, and is also excellent preparation for what follows: an extension of the role-playing technique involving multiple players.

Romeo and Juliet is the world's most famous love story. Shakespeare's appeal has seen his plays and poems translated into every language on the planet. Most adult students will be familiar with, or at least have some background knowledge of the "star-crossed lovers." However, even without this background knowledge, the reworking of Shakespeare's classic that appears below is clear, simple, and doesn't require much explanation.

By moving chairs and desks to create a performance space, assigning roles, and perhaps prefacing the role play with a discussion about the characters and their attributes (and of course by giving students a chance to connect with their inner thespian), the aim of *Romeo and Juliet*: The Ten Minute ESL Version is to create a sense of fun, while involving students in a storytelling process that is underpinned by spoken language.

By encouraging students to concentrate on the playing of the drama, and to follow character's basic objectives through their acting, "intention" not "pronunciation" is center stage, which for some students may be the key to unlocking speech inhibition.

The classical text has been simplified and "translated" into contemporary English language. This serves the practical aim of facilitating a clear understanding of the story in its native source, while preparing students for any further learning activities related to the material. These may include exploring the original text of Shakespeare's plays and poetry, classroom discussion or writing exercises about the story and/or the acting process involved in telling it.

Romeo and Juliet: The Ten Minute ESL Version

Scene 1

A public place. Enter ROMEO (of the MONTAGUE family) from one side of the stage and TYBALT (of the CAPULET family) from the opposite side of the stage.

They circle each other.

ROMEO: Are you making a rude gesture at me, sir?

TYBALT: No, sir, I am not making a rude gesture at you, sir, but I am making a rude gesture.

They draw their swords and fight. Enter old MONTAGUE and CAPULET on opposing sides. They draw their swords and fight. Enter more people from both families, fighting, including BENVOLIO. Enter the PRINCE and servants.

PRINCE: Rebels! Enemies of peace! Can't they hear me? Hey! You men, you animals! Stop!

The fighting stops.

If ever you disturb our streets again, you will pay with your lives.

Exit the PRINCE followed by everyone except BENVOILIO and ROMEO.

BENVOLIO: Good morning, cousin. Why are you so sad?

ROMEO: Because I don't have the thing I want.

BENVOLIO: Ah! You are in love?

ROMEO: Out.

BENVOLIO: Of love?

ROMEO: I love her but she doesn't love me.

BENVOLIO: Listen to me. Don't think about her. Let your eyes look at other girls.

ROMEO: But people who are blinded by love cannot forget the wonderful thing they can't see anymore. I'm going. You can't teach me to forget her.

BENVOLIO: Yes I can or I'll die trying.

They go.

Scene 2

Enter PARIS, CAPULET and CLOWN.

PARIS: My lord, tell me what you think of my proposal.

CAPULET: My child is too young to get married to you. She's not even fourteen yet.

PARIS: I've seen mothers younger than her.

CAPULET: Young mothers always have such tough lives. But listen, I'm not saying, "No" completely. Be charming, gentle Paris, get her heart, and if she falls in love with you, I'll agree to your proposal to marry her. (*To CLOWN)* Travel through Verona, and find the people written on this list.

Gives him a list.

Invite them to our party.

Exit CAPULET and PARIS. CLOWN remains. He studies the list but he cannot read. Enter ROMEO and BENVOLIO.

CLOWN: Excuse me, sir, can you read this?

ROMEO: Yes, if I understand the letters and the language.

ROMEO studies the list.

Wow! There are some very important people on this list. What is this invitation for?

CLOWN: My master is the rich Capulet, and if you are not related to the Montague family, I invite you to come and drink wine with us tonight. Goodbye.

He goes.

BENVOLIO: That girl Rosaline, the one you love is going to be at the Capulet's party. Compare her face to some other girls I'll show you, and I'll make you think your swan is actually a crow.

ROMEO: I'll go along, not because I believe you are right, but because I want to see Rosaline, the girl I love.

They go.

Scene 3

CAPULET's house. Enter LADY CAPULET and NURSE.

LADY CAPULET: Nurse, where's my daughter? Tell her to come here.

NURSE: Goodness! Where is the girl? *(Calling)* Juliet!

Enter JULIET.

JULIET: I'm here. What do you want?

LADY CAPULET: What do you think about getting married? The handsome Paris wants you to be his wife. You'll meet him tonight at our party.

JULIET: I'll check him out, and if I like him, I like him.

Enter SERVANT.

SERVANT: Madam, the guests are here.

LADY CAPULET: You go first Juliet and we'll follow you. Paris is waiting.

NURSE: Go, girl, and find a man who'll make you happy.

They exit.

Scene 4

The hall in CAPULET's house. Three friends: ROMEO, MERCUTIO, and BENVOLIO put on masks and enter the hall. Enter CAPULET.

CAPULET: Welcome, Gentlemen!

Music plays. The guests dance.

ROMEO: *(To SERVANT)* Who is the lady over there holding that guy's hand?

SERVINGMAN: I don't know sir.

ROMEO: Wow! She shows the lights how to be bright!

TYBALT: I hear the voice of a Montague. Fetch me my sword, boy.

His servant goes.

CAPULET: What's up nephew? Why are you so angry?

TYBALT: Uncle, that man in the mask is a Montague, our enemy. This lowlife comes here out of hatred, to make fun of us and our party.

CAPULET: It's Romeo, isn't it? Don't worry about him, he's harmless. Just leave him alone.

TYBALT: Well, I do worry about it, and I won't put up with him being here.

CAPULET: You will do what I tell you to do because this is my house and I expect you to do what I want, you cheeky young man!

TYBALT exits. ROMEO takes JULIET's hand.

ROMEO: Your hand is like a temple that my hand is not good enough to visit, but my lips are like two blushing visitors at the temple, ready to make things better with a kiss.

He kisses her hand.

NURSE: Madam, your mother wants to talk to you. Listen, young man, her mother is the lady of this house.

ROMEO: What a price to pay! My life is in my enemy's hand.

MERCUTIO: Come on, let's go, the fun is over.

ROMEO: I think you're right. If we stay longer things will only get worse.

ROMEO, MERCUTIO, and BENVOLIO exit.

NURSE: *(To JULIET)* His name is Romeo and he is a member of the Montague family. He is the only son of the Capulet's greatest enemy.

JULIET: My only love is the son of my only hate! I met him before I knew his name, and when I found out his name it was too late!

Exit.

Scene 5

CAPULET's orchard. Enter ROMEO alone. JULIET appears on the balcony of her bedroom on the second floor of the house.

ROMEO: What's that light shining from the window up there?

JULIET: O Romeo, Romeo! Where are you Romeo?

ROMEO: I'm here Juliet. With love's light wings, I flew over the walls. Ha! One high, stone wall cannot keep my love out.

JULIET: If they find you here, they'll kill you.

ROMEO: This black cloak will hide me.

JULIET: What satisfaction can you get by coming here tonight?

ROMEO: If you tell me that you love me, I'll tell you the same. Then I'll be satisfied.

Noises inside the house.

JULIET: If you are telling me the truth, and you want to marry me, I'll send someone to find you tomorrow and you can give them a message to give to me.

ROMEO: Okay. Send someone to see me at nine o'clock.

JULIET: Goodnight, goodnight, but saying goodbye is so sad.

ROMEO: Sleep well, have a peaceful night! I wish I were Sleep and Peace, then I could spend the night with you.

They exit.

Scene 6

A public place the following morning. Enter NURSE and ROMEO.

NURSE: My young lady told me to find you.

ROMEO: Nurse, send her my best wishes. Tell her to find some way to leave the house this afternoon and come to Friar Lawrence's place. We'll get married there in secret. Here's some money for the hard work you are doing.

NURSE: Okay, I'll do it.

Scene 7

Enter FRIAR LAWRENCE with JULIET.

FRIAR: Come with me Juliet. We will make quick work of this. I'm not going to leave you and Romeo alone together, until you are married.

Scene 8

Enter ROMEO's friends, MERCUTIO and BENVOLIO from one side of the stage. Enter TYBALT and others from the opposite side of the stage.

BENVOLIO: Look! Here come the Capulets.

MERCUTIO: Let them come. I don't care.

TYBALT: Stay close to me. I'm going to talk to them. Excuse me, gentlemen, I'd like to say something.

MERCUTIO: You want to talk to us? You can talk to us if you like and you can fight with us too!

BENVOLIO: We are in a public place. Go somewhere private to sort out this problem, or just go. Here, everyone is watching.

Enter ROMEO, married.

TYBALT: Don't worry about it, sirs, here's the man I want to see. Romeo, the love I have for you is no better than what I'm about to tell you: you are a villain.

MERCUTIO draws his sword.

MERCUTIO: Tybalt, you rat catcher, do you want to fight me?

TYBALT: Sure. I'll fight you.

TYBALT draws his sword.

ROMEO: Gentle Mercutio, put your sword away.

MERCUTIO: Come, sir, show me your best sword moves.

They fight.

ROMEO: Take your sword out Benvolio, beat down their weapons. Stop, Tybalt! Stop, good Mercutio!

TYBALT stabs MERCUTIO with his sword. TYBALT flees.

MERCUTIO: Help me, Benvolio, or I will faint. I wish both your families would catch the plague!

MERCUTIO dies.

BENVOLIO: O Romeo, Romeo, brave Mercutio is dead.

ROMEO: This terrible day is the start of more terrible days to come.

TYBALT returns, sword drawn. ROMEO draws, they fight, ROMEO kills TYBALT.

ROMEO: I think I am the unluckiest man alive.

BENVOLIO: Why are you still here? Go!

ROMEO exits. Enter citizens and PRINCE ESCALUS.

PRINCE: Benvolio, who began this bloody fight?

BENVOLIO: Tybalt, started all the trouble by killing Mercutio. Then Romeo killed Tybalt.

PRINCE: Tybalt killed Mercutio and Romeo killed Tybalt. These two men lost their lives and Romeo will lose his life if he ever returns to this city. My word is final. I won't listen to your pleading and begging. Your tears won't persuade me either.

They go.

Scene 9

FRIAR LAWRENCE's hut.

ROMEO: Friar, what's the news? What is the prince's decision?

FRIAR: You are banned from the city forever.

ROMEO: There is no world outside of Verona for me, only Hell itself.

Knocking at the door.

FRIAR: Run to my study and hide.

More knocking.

For God's sake, hide. Why are you being so stupid!

NURSE: *(From outside)* Let me come in and I'll tell you why I'm here. I come from Lady Juliet.

FRIAR: Welcome then.

Enter NURSE.

NURSE: Where is my lady's husband? Where's Romeo?

FRIAR: There on the ground like someone drunk on their own tears.

NURSE: Juliet is exactly the same.

FRIAR: Cheer up man! Your Juliet is alive. Climb up to her bedroom, and comfort her. But do it before the city gates are closed, because if you are too late you won't be able to escape to Mantua, where you will live and wait for the right time to make your marriage public, stop your families from fighting, get the Prince to pardon you, and bring you back home.

NURSE: My lord, I'll tell my lady you are coming.

ROMEO: Please do, and tell her to prepare all the bad things she has to say to me.

NURSE: Here, sir, she told me to give you this ring.

She goes.

ROMEO: This ring cheers me up so much.

FRIAR: Give me your hand. It's late. Goodbye, goodnight.

They go.

Scene 10

CAPULET's house. Enter CAPULET, his wife, and PARIS.

PARIS: These sad times are not the time for love.

CAPULET: What does my child think about love? She will do exactly what I tell her. I have no doubts about that. Wife, go and tell her before you go to bed that on Thursday, she will get married to this noble man, Paris.

PARIS: My lord, I wish Thursday were tomorrow.

Scene 11

JULIET's bedroom. ROMEO and JULIET stand at the window.

JULIET: Are you going? It's still a long time before dawn.

ROMEO: I heard the song of a morning bird. I must go, and live, or stay and die.

JULIET: You had better go then! It's getting lighter.

ROMEO: More daylight, more darkness and sadness for us.

They kiss. He lowers the ladder and descends.

LADY CAPULET: *(Outside the door)* Daughter, are you up?

She enters.

How are you Juliet? Still crying over your cousin's death? Don't you worry, we'll get revenge. But listen, I have some very happy news my girl. Early next Thursday morning, you will marry the County Paris at Saint Peter's Church.

JULIET: I won't get married yet, and when I do, I swear it will be Romeo, who you know I hate, rather than Paris. You call this happy news!

LADY CAPULET: Here comes your father, tell him yourself.

Enter CAPULET.

CAPULET: Have you told her what we've decided?

JULIET: Good father, I'm begging you on my knees, don't make me marry Paris.

CAPULET: Listen, you had better get to the church on Thursday or never look at me again.

CAPULET and LADY CAPULET leave.

JULIET: I'll go and see the friar, he'll know what to do and if he can't help me, I'll kill myself.

Scene 12

Enter FRIAR.

FRIAR: Take this small bottle of poison, drink it, and immediately you will feel a cold sleepiness running through your veins. Your pulse will be so weak that everyone will think you are dead. You will continue to appear dead for forty-two hours. Then you'll wake up, and feel like you've just had a pleasant sleep. I'll send Romeo a letter and tell him about our plan, then he'll come here and we'll watch you wake up, and that very night Romeo will take you away to Mantua.

He gives her the poison and leaves.

JULIET: Romeo, I'm coming. I drink this for you.

She drinks from the bottle. She falls on the bed.

Scene 13

Mantua. A street with stores. Enter ROMEO followed by BALTHASAR.

ROMEO: Hi Balthasar. What's the news from Verona? How is my wife?

BALTHASAR: I'm so sorry to bring bad news, but her body sleeps in the cemetery.

ROMEO: What? Is it possible? I curse the stars! Don't you have a letter from the friar?

BALTHASAR: No, my good lord.

ROMEO: It doesn't matter. Just go away and leave me alone.

BALTHASAR goes.

Hey you, pharmacist!

Enter PHARMACIST.

Here is forty ducats, now give me some poison, some fast-acting stuff that will travel through the veins so quickly that when a suicidal person takes it, they will die instantly.

ROMEO gives him the money. The PHARMACIST gives ROMEO a bottle of poison.

Scene 14

Verona. FRIAR LAWRENCE's cell. Enter FRIAR JOHN.

FRIAR: Welcome back from Mantua Friar John. What did Romeo say about my letter? Or, if he wrote down his reply, give me his letter.

FRIAR JOHN: This is the letter you told me to give to Romeo. I couldn't deliver it because I was locked up inside a house in a small town near Mantua. The townspeople thought the house might be infected by the plague, so my trip to the city was cancelled.

Scene 15

Verona. The CAPULETS tomb inside the graveyard.

PARIS: My sweet flower, here are some more flowers for your

bed. How sad, your roof is dust and stones!

A noise.

Who is that wandering around the graveyard tonight?

Enter ROMEO. He begins to open the tomb.

Stop your unholy work, horrible Montague!

ROMEO: Are you trying to make me angry? Let's fight then, boy!

They fight. ROMEO stabs PARIS.

PARIS: O, I am injured! *(He falls)* If you have any mercy, open the tomb, and lay me with Juliet.

PARIS dies.

ROMEO: Okay, I will, whoever you are. Let me look at his face. Mercutio's relative, the noble County Paris! Dead man, lie there, and you'll be buried by a dead man called Romeo.

He lays PARIS in the tomb. He goes to where JULIET lies.

Eyes, take a last look at her! Arms, take a last hug! And lips, with your last kiss you sign the deal I have done with Death! Here's to my love! *(He drinks)* Oh honest pharmacist! Your drugs are quick. So with a kiss, I die.

ROMEO dies. Enter FRIAR LAWRENCE.

FRIAR: Romeo? Dead? Who else? What? Paris is dead too? Oh no, the lady is waking up.

Juliet wakes.

JULIET: Dear friar, where is my husband?

Voices approach from the distance.

FRIAR: I hear some noises, lady. Let's get out of this dreadful place first.

She sees ROMEO's body.

JULIET: Go! Get out! Leave! I'll never go!

FRIAR leaves.

What's this? A cup, held in my lover's hand? He took the poison. I can see that now.

Noises off.

Noises? Then I'll be quick. Come happy dagger, my stomach is your sheath.

She stabs herself with Romeo's knife.

There rest and let me die.

She dies. Enter the PRINCE followed by people of the town.

PRINCE: What terrible things have happened here that get me out of my bed so early in the morning?

He sees the bodies and talks to the CAPULETS and MONTAGUES who have followed him into the tomb.

Look at the evil your hatred has caused. Heaven has killed your joys with love!

CAPULET: Brother Montague, give me your hand. That is all I can offer you. I cannot give you anything else.

MONTAGUE: But I can give you more. I will build a statue of your daughter in pure gold, so that as long as this city exists, there will be no one in it so highly praised than the true and faithful Juliet.

CAPULET: The statue of Romeo that I will build next to Juliet's will be just as great. Our fighting has caused such terrible sacrifices!

PRINCE: Let's go now and talk some more about these sad things. There was never a story of more woe, than this story about Juliet and her Romeo.

Love Is In The Air

Finally, (and continuing the theme of Love), let's take a look at one of the English language's most famous love poems, Shakespeare's Sonnet 18, "Shall I compare thee to a summer's day?"

It appears below in the original text, and then followed by my modern translation of the text for ESL learners.

Shall I compare thee to a summer's day?
Thou art more lovely and more temperate.
Rough winds do shake the darling buds of May,
And summer's lease hath all too short a date.
Sometime too hot the eye of heaven shines,
And often is his gold complexion dimmed,
And every fair from fair sometime declines,
By chance or nature's changing course untrimmed;
But thy eternal summer shall not fade
Nor lose possession of that fair thou ow'st,
Nor shall death brag thou wand'rest in his shade
When in eternal lines to Time thou grow'st.
So long as men can breathe, or eyes can see,
So long lives this, and this gives life to thee.

Shall I compare you to a summer's day?
You are more lovely and much milder too.
In May, the flower buds are shaken by the winds,
And summer never lasts that long at all,
Sometimes, it's far too hot,
Sometimes, the sun is hidden by the clouds.
All things lose their beauty in the end,
By chance, or age,
But your everlasting summer will never fade,
Nor lose the beauty that you own,
And Death won't brag you walk with him
When my poetry keeps you young.
So long as men can breathe or eyes can see,
This poem lives, and it gives life to you.

Afterword

The ESL classroom is a place where a great deal of time is spent on all the practical bits of English; the building blocks of language that are well-represented by grammar and vocabulary, and which when put together in the correct fashion allow thoughts and ideas to be freely expressed.

Whether the ESL student wishes to get ahead in business or simply perform a basic task at the bank or restaurant, the ESL quest is so often concerned with all the day to day language practicalities that seem to govern our lives.

For many immigrants whose second language is English, mastery of such skills will keep them afloat in a sea of English language, and ultimately, help them to steer a course through the English-speaking world.

The very idea of learning the language simply for the love of English, its unique sound and feel; its idiosyncrasies and rhythms, is an idea that might be given **short shrift** by some language students and their ESL teachers. Some might even view such an approach as a folly; something for the hobbyists back in the safety of their native land, from where they can "play" with language **to their heart's content**.

However, my aim in writing this book, and with the help of an irreverent and fun approach to Shakespeare and the world of ESL, is to provide the ESL student with a thorough grounding in some practical, everyday phrases and idioms in my mother tongue.

At the same time, I hope to have offered a glimpse of Shakespeare that may whet the student's appetite for more. If we wish to learn some of the finer points of the language, we really could have no better teacher than a writer who is widely regarded as the greatest to have ever lived.

There are of course, far easier places to start an exploration of English literature. Furthermore, it is true to say that Shakespeare is not going help the ESL student order breakfast in the local café nor arm the student with some friendly conversation starters.

It is a fact that countless words Shakespeare put to good use have long since fallen out of favor with English speakers around the world. Not even the Queen of England uses a "thee" or "thou" in the twenty-first century.

Nevertheless, Shakespeare remains the master not just of literature but of the spoken word. He was a thoroughly practical man who wrote plays to be performed and words to be spoken aloud. There is a richness to Shakespeare's words that even in condensed idiomatic form is something special.

Should you choose to explore Shakespeare further, the sonnets are a good place to start. In fourteen lines, Shakespeare gave the English language 154 love poems, which explore the gamut of human emotion.

There are countless books available on Shakespeare's poetry and plays but perhaps the most useful for the ESL student are those that offer a side-by-side "translation." That is, the original text alongside a contemporary text in modern English.

Whatever you choose to do next with the English language, I encourage you to keep a sense of fun and positivity in all you do, and approach learning with a spirit of inquiry. Good luck!

Quick List

1. All's well that ends well.
2. All one to me.
3. All that glitters is not gold.
4. As dead as a doornail.
5. As good luck would have it.
6. As pure as the driven snow.
7. Bated breath.
8. Be all and end all.
9. Bear a charmed life.
10. Brave new world.
11. Beggar all description.
12. Break the ice.
13. Brevity is the soul of wit.
14. Cold comfort.
15. Come full circle.
16. Come what come may.
17. (The course of) true love never did run smooth.
18. Cruel to be kind.
19. Dash to pieces.
20. Devil incarnate.
21. A dish fit for the gods.
22. Done to death.
23. Eaten out of house and home.
24. Elbow room.
25. Eyesore.
26. Faint-hearted.
27. Fair play.
28. Fancy-free.
29. Fight fire with fire.
30. Fool's paradise.
31. Foregone conclusion.
32. Forever and a day.
33. Foul play.
34. The game is up.
35. Gild the lily.
36. Good riddance.
37. Green-eyed monster.
38. Halcyon days.

39. Heart's content.
40. High time.
41. Hot-blooded.
42. Improbable fiction.
43. In pickle.
44. In my heart of hearts.
45. In my mind's eye.
46. In stitches.
47. It's Greek to me.
48. It smells to heaven.
49. Kill with kindness.
50. Knock, knock! Who's there?
51. The lady doth protest too much, methinks.
52. Laid on with a trowel.
53. Laughing stock.
54. Lie low.
55. Love is blind.
56. Melt into thin air.
57. Method in his madness.
58. More fool you.
59. Much ado about nothing.
60. Neither a borrower nor a lender be.
61. Neither here nor there.
62. Neither rhyme nor reason.
63. Night owl.
64. Not slept a wink.
65. One fell swoop.
66. Own flesh and blood.
67. Pitched battle.
68. Play fast and loose.
69. Pomp and circumstance.
70. Pound of flesh.
71. The Queen's English.
72. Refuse to budge and inch.
73. Salad days.
74. Sea change.
75. Seen better days.
76. Send someone packing.
77. Set one's teeth on edge.
78. The short and long of it.
79. Short shrift.
80. Sorry sight.

81. Something rotten in the state of Denmark.
82. Spotless reputation.
83. Stony hearted.
84. Strange bedfellows.
85. That way madness lies.
86. Thereby hangs a tale.
87. Throw cold water on it.
88. To be or not to be.
89. Too much of a good thing.
90. Tongue-tied.
91. To the manner born.
92. To thine own self be true.
93. A tower of strength.
94. Truth will out.
95. Up in arms.
96. Vanish into thin air.
97. Wear my heart upon my sleeve.
98. What a piece of work is man!
99. What's done is done.
100. Wild goose chase.
101. The world's my oyster.

Quick Quiz Answer Key

Quick Quiz 1

1. FALSE
2. FALSE
3. TRUE
4. TRUE
5. FALSE
6. FALSE
7. FALSE
8. TRUE
9. TRUE
10. TRUE

Quick Quiz 2

1. Break the ice.
2. Beggars all description.
3. Come full circle.
4. Cruel to be kind.
5. Come what come may.
6. Brevity is the soul of wit.
7. Dashed to pieces.
8. Cold comfort.
9. The course of true love never did run smooth.
10. Devil incarnate.

Quick Quiz 3

1. Elbow room.
2. A dish fit for the gods.
3. An eyesore.
4. Fancy-free.
5. Faint hearted.
6. Done to death.
7. Fight fire with fire.
8. Fair play.
9. Fool's paradise.
10. Eaten out of house and home.

Quick Quiz 4

1. The game is UP.
2. FOUL play.
3. GOOD riddance.
4. GREEN-eyed monster.
5. Halcyon DAYS.
6. HIGH time.
7. GILD the lily.
8. FOREGONE conclusion.
9. FOREVER and a day.
10. To one's heart's CONTENT.

Quick Quiz 5

1. C	6. D
2. A	7. B
3. D	8. B
4. C	9. C
5. C	10. A

Quick Quiz 6

1. FALSE	6. FALSE
2. TRUE	7. TRUE
3. FALSE	8. TRUE
4. TRUE	9. FALSE
5. FALSE	10. TRUE

Quick Quiz 7

1. Not slept a wink.
2. Night owl.
3. Pomp and circumstance.
4. Pitched battle.
5. Own flesh and blood.
6. Pound of flesh.
7. Fast and loose.
8. One fell swoop.
9. Neither here nor there.
10. Neither rhyme nor reason.

Quick Quiz 8

1. Send (someone) packing.
2. Refuse to budge an inch.
3. Seen better days.
4. The Queen's English.
5. Short shrift.
6. Something rotten in the state of Denmark.
7. A sea change.
8. The short and the long of it.
9. Set one's teeth on edge.
10. Salad days.

Quick Quiz 9

1. A sorry sight.
2. Throw cold water on it.
3. Strange bedfellows.
4. Thereby hangs a tale.
5. That way madness lies.
6. A spotless reputation.
7. To be or not to be.
8. Stony hearted.
9. Tongue-tied.
10. Too much of a good thing.

Quick Quiz 10

1. D
2. B
3. C
4. A
5. C
6. A
7. B
8. D
9. C
10. B
11. B

Biography

Photo by: Isar Jamalpour—www.isarphotography.com

Martin Jago is an interdiciplinary theatre practitioner, director, and acting coach from Great Britain who specializes in Shakespeare and the retelling of classical texts. He trained as an actor at The Royal Welsh College of Music and Drama and over the course of several decades has developed into a multi-faceted theatre professional who employs bold and imaginative approaces to the actor's craft and the storytelling process.

Passionate about actor training and education, he has instructed thousands of student actors and professionals alike. He lives in Los Angeles and works internationally.

His first book, *To Play or Not To Play: 50 Games for Acting Shakespeare* was published in 2012 by Smith and Kraus